cooking of the
caribbean

cooking of the
caribbean

TROPICAL TASTE SENSATIONS
FROM THE ISLANDS IN THE SUN

ROSAMUND GRANT

LORENZ BOOKS

To my brothers and sisters: Leyland, Bernie, Waveney and Paula,
who constantly give me love and support

This edition published by Lorenz Books

© Anness Publishing Limited 1995, 1999

Lorenz Books is an imprint of Anness Publishing Limited
Hermes House, 88–89 Blackfriars Road, London SE1 8HA

This edition distributed in Canada by Raincoast Books
8680 Cambie Street, Vancouver, British Columbia V6P 6M9

ISBN 0-7548-0265-5

A CIP catalogue record for this book is available from the British Library

Publisher: Joanna Lorenz
Senior Cookery Editor: Linda Fraser
Cookery Editor: Anne Hildyard
Copy Editor: Christine Ingram
Designer: Siân Keogh
Photography and styling: Patrick McLeavey, assisted by Rebecca Sturrock
Food for Photography: Joanne Craig assisted by Curtis Edwards
Illustrator: Madeleine David

Front Cover: William Lingwood, Photographer; Helen Trent, Stylist;
Sunil Vijayakar, Home Economist

Printed in Hong Kong/China

1 3 5 7 9 10 8 6 4 2

ACKNOWLEDGEMENTS
The author wishes to thank Chandis for all her hard work typing the
manuscript, Gale for help with the Barbadian Coconut Sweet Bread, and her children Joanna,
Nayo and Chris, for all their practical help.

Pictures on page 1 and top right page 7: Zefa Pictures Ltd
Pictures on pages 2, 3 and bottom left page 7: Greg Evans International Photo Library

NOTES
For all recipes, quantities are given in both metric and imperial measures and, where appropriate,
measures are also given in standard cups and spoons. Follow one set, but not a mixture because
they are not interchangeable.

Standard spoon and cup measurements are level.
1 tbsp = 15ml, 1 tsp = 5ml, 1 cup = 250ml/8fl oz

Australian standard tablespoons are 20ml. Australian readers should use 3 tsp in place of 1 tbsp
for measuring small quantities of gelatine, cornflour, salt etc.

Medium eggs should be used unless otherwise stated.

CONTENTS

INTRODUCTION

Cooking of the Caribbean features recipes that reflect the rich diversity of traditions and culture that is the hallmark of the Caribbean. People of many different races and cultures have lived in the Caribbean islands over the centuries, and their presence changed not only the history of the islands, but also profoundly influenced its cuisine. With each set of people came their traditional cooking methods, they imported their own favourite foods, planting fruit and vegetables and rearing livestock. Gradually over the years the various islanders embraced these traditions as their own and today we have to realise that what we think of as Caribbean cooking, is actually a blend of food and cookery traditions from all over the world.

The first inhabitants of the Caribbean were the Arawak Indians who sailed from the Americas. They surely must have thought they had found paradise in these islands, with fresh fish from the seas, and yams, sweet potatoes, paw paws, pineapples and guavas growing in abundance.

Jerked pork, a traditional Caribbean dish, where the whole pig is spit roasted over a slow fire is almost certainly of Arawak tradition. The Arawaks were skilled hunters and fishermen, they cultivated crops, chiefly cassava, from which they derived a variety of products and they were renowned for their intricately designed and attractively patterned arts and crafts.

The Europeans, who colonised the region in the early sixteenth century, also had a significant influence. They experimented with the cultivation of bananas, plantains, coconut, sugar cane, oranges, limes and ginger – crops that then were new to the island, and today we think of as essentially Caribbean. Along with sugar cane, cotton and coffee began to be grown on plantations for the export trade.

The tropical islands of the Caribbean stretch from the coast of South America out into the Atlantic ocean.

Cod, which had been salted and stored in the ship's hold on its long journey from Europe to the New World, would have been among the foods introduced about this time. The Europeans, having virtually exterminated the Arawaks, introduced slave labour to work in the plantations and over the years millions of Africans were brought to the islands. The slaves were forbidden to raise cattle and frequently prevented from eating fresh fish or meat, so they came to depend on salted fish. They acquired a great liking for it and saltfish has remained popular, inspite of the availability of so much fresh fish.

Although the Africans were initially not allowed their traditional foods, yams, okra and ackee were later brought from Africa. They retained their traditional cooking style and were renowned for their culinary skills.

For most slaves, their diet was bland and monotonous and it was they who made the most of the island's pungent spices and seasonings to flavour their broths and stews. When slavery was abolished in 1830, plantation owners looked elsewhere for labour and found it among people from the Middle East, India and China. They came as indentured labourers and traders and

Picking out the perfect ingredient from a market stall in Martinique (below) or from trays heaped with chillies (right).

brought with them a wealth of new customs, cooking styles and foods.

Thus out of this turbulent past comes a cuisine that is colourful and versatile, imaginative and abounding in creativity. My style of cooking acknowledges the roots of our food culture and celebrates the talents of its cooks. The recipes here have been developed using traditional styles and ingredients in contemporary ways. The Caribbean is renowned for its liberal use of spices and herbs, and for marinating and seasoning meat and fish. The waters are a paradise of tropical fish and shellfish, while fresh vegetables, fragrant herbs and spices grow in profusion. Tropical fruits and vegetables are ideal for vegetarians, offering interesting texture and flavour. Yams, sweet potatoes and other staples go well with spicy tomato-based sauces. Okra and

pumpkin, when stir-fried with shellfish, make delicious, quick and easy lunches, while mangoes and pineapple add that special touch to fruit salads and drinks. Of course, our sugar cane crops produce potent rum that make splendid punches and cocktails which are always enjoyed by visitors to the islands. Our custom is always to have a little something in the fridge or cupboard, such as ice-cold fruity lemonade and patties or luscious ice cream – just in case a visitor or friend pops in. Caribbean housewives enjoy entertaining at home and prefer it to dining out. Our buffets usually cater for all tastes, including faddy children or non-meat eaters. I hope this cookery book will enable you to bring the delights of the Caribbean kitchen to your friends, families and guests and encourage you to create your own tastes of the Caribbean.

INGREDIENTS

The following ingredients are typically used in Caribbean cooking. Some may be unfamiliar, but they are all available in supermarkets and shops selling Caribbean foods. Commercial blends of herbs and spices can be used to season meat and fish, or try a home-made mixture; spice seasoning and herb seasoning.

ACKEE

This is the fruit of an evergreen tree. The texture is soft, resembling scrambled eggs and it has a slightly lemony flavour. Traditionally served with saltfish, it is also delicious with prawns or vegetables. It is available, canned, from Caribbean stores.

AUBERGINE

There are many varieties – large, purple and oval-shaped, small and round, or thin and pale purple. In west Africa, the small, round, white aubergines are known as garden eggs or eggplant.

BEANS AND PEAS

These include black-eyed beans, red kidney beans, black beans, pigeon peas (gunga peas) and various coloured lentils. They are often combined with rice or used in soups and stews.

Clockwise from top left: cooked king prawns, saltfish (dried salted cod), red bream, small red snappers and cooked prawns.

CASSAVA

This tropical root vegetable originated in Brazil, and was introduced to Africa at the beginning of the 17th century. It is a long irregularly shaped root vegetable with a rough brown skin and hard white starchy flesh. A popular vegetable in the Caribbean, it can be eaten boiled, baked or fried.

Clockwise from top left: large and small avocados, limes, guavas, pineapple, large mangoes and small mangoes.

CHRISTOPHENE

Also known as cho-cho or chayote, this pear-shaped vegetable has a bland flavour and is similar in texture to squash. It is cooked and used as a side dish or in soups.

COCONUT

This is a large one-seeded nut of the coconut palm tree. The mature coconut has a hairy outer shell containing sweet thick white flesh, from which coconut milk is extracted. Chop into small pieces then liquidize with a little water and press through a sieve to extract the milk.

CREAMED COCONUT

Commercially made, creamed coconut can be bought in 200g/7oz packets from most supermarkets, grocery and health food shops. The coconut can be stored for several weeks in the fridge, for use in recipes.

CORNMEAL

Cornmeal is made from dried ground corn kernels. The type most commonly used is yellow – either fine or coarse-grained. Cornmeal can be used to make cakes, breads and porridge or as a coating for frying fish or chicken.

DHAL

In the Caribbean, this is a spicy soup made from split peas or lentils. Dhal puri (or roti) is an unleavened bread.

EDDOE OR COCO

A small globular root vegetable, related to the dasheen. The flesh is white and starchy like potato and after peeling can either be boiled and served as an accompaniment to stews or in soup.

Clockwise from top left: okra, christophene, baby aubergines, aubergine, garden eggs and ackee.

GREEN BANANAS

Only certain varieties are used in cooking. They are usually boiled, with or without their skins. Widely available in Caribbean shops.

Clockwise from top left: cassava, eddoes, orange sweet potatoes, white yam and white sweet potatoes.

Clockwise from top left: green plantains, coconut, ripe yellow plantains and green bananas.

GUAVA

The pale yellow edible skin covers rose-pink succulent flesh, which in turn covers a seed-laden soft pulp. Guavas have a slightly spiced smell and are used to make jam and jelly or added to fruit salads.

HERB SEASONING

Pound 4 chopped spring onions, 1 garlic clove, 15ml/1 tbsp each fresh or 5ml/1 tsp dried, thyme and basil with 15ml/1 tbsp fresh coriander, in a mortar until smooth.

MANGOES

Mangoes come in a variety of shapes, sizes, colours and textures. Unripe, they are green, turning yellow, pink or crimson-green as they ripen. For desserts, jellies or jams, make sure the fruit is ripe – it should feel pliable to the touch without being too spongy. Unripe, green mangoes are used for chutney, curries and stews.

OKRA

Okra is used widely in Caribbean cookery. Avoid larger varieties and choose small, firm ones. Wash and dry before trimming and cutting to prevent them from getting too sticky.

PEPPERS

The *Capsicum frutescens* family includes hot and sweet peppers and there are many varieties of hot peppers – or chillies. Fresh chillies can be green, red or yellow. The seeds and core are the hottest part and can be removed before use, under cold running water. A wide variety of peppers is grown in the Caribbean. One of the hottest is the "Scotch Bonnet" pepper. It's best to wear gloves when preparing peppers. Take care not to rub your eyes afterwards.

PLANTAINS

These are a member of the banana family. They are inedible raw and must be cooked before eating. They can be green, yellow or very dark according to ripeness and can be roasted, boiled, mashed and fried. Plantains can be eaten as an appetizer, in soups, as a vegetable or in desserts.

SALTFISH OR SALT COD

Of all the saltfish, cod has the best flavour. To remove the salt, wash well and soak for several hours or overnight in cold water, then remove the fish to clean water and boil for 15–20 minutes. Discard the water. Flake the fish, discarding the skin and bones.

Clockwise from top left: red kidney beans, fresh pigeon peas, dried pigeon peas, yellow split peas, butter beans, split red lentils and cornmeal (centre).

Clockwise from top: red pepper, red and orange Scotch Bonnet peppers, small green and red chillies, sweet green peppers, Scotch Bonnet peppers and large green and red chillies.

SNAPPER OR RED FISH

A silver, pinkish-red fish with firm white flesh, snapper is imported in small or large sizes from approximately 225g–1.5kg/8oz–3lb. Snapper can be fried, baked, steamed or boiled.

SPICE SEASONING

Mix 15ml/1 tbsp garlic granules, 7.5ml/½ tbsp coarse-grain black pepper, 7.5ml/½ tbsp each paprika, celery salt and curry powder with 5ml/1 tsp caster sugar. Store in a dry container.

SWEET POTATO

The skin of this vegetable ranges in colour from white to pink to reddish brown. The white-fleshed, red-skinned variety is most commonly used in Caribbean cooking. Sweet potatoes can be boiled, roasted, fried, creamed or baked in their skins – and are used in sweet and savoury dishes.

YAM

These come in all sizes – some varieties are huge – so when buying, ask for a piece the size you need. The flesh is either yellow or white and can be eaten boiled, roasted, baked, mashed or made into chips or fu fu.

SOUPS
AND
STARTERS

In the Caribbean, soup can be either a starter or a meal in itself. Time and effort is often spent making good rich stocks from meat and fish which become the base for a family meal. However, for a first course, lighter soups, like Creamy Spinach Soup, and Fish and Sweet Potato Soup, are ideal being both simple and tasty. Snacks not only make delicious accompaniments to drinks, they are also excellent as starters or can be served at picnics or parties. Spinach patties are my version of the more traditional minced meat patties.

Creamy Spinach Soup

An appetizing soup that you will find yourself making over and over again.

INGREDIENTS

Serves 4

25g/1oz/2 tbsp butter
1 small onion, chopped
675g/1½ lb fresh spinach, chopped
1.2 litres/2 pints/5 cups vegetable stock
50g/2oz creamed coconut
freshly grated nutmeg
300ml/½ pint/1¼ cups single cream
salt and freshly ground black pepper
fresh snipped chives, to garnish

1 Melt the butter in a saucepan over a moderate heat and sauté the onion for a few minutes until soft. Add the spinach, cover the pan and cook gently for 10 minutes, until the spinach has reduced.

2 Pour the spinach mixture into a blender or food processor and add a little of the stock. Blend until smooth.

3 Return mixture to the pan and add the remaining stock, creamed coconut, salt, pepper and nutmeg. Simmer for 15 minutes to thicken.

4 Add the cream, stir well and heat through – do not boil. Serve hot, garnished with chives.

COOK'S TIP

If fresh spinach is not available, use frozen. Milk can be substituted for the cream – in which case, use half stock and half milk.

Beef Broth with Cassava

This simple, tasty "big", soup is almost like a stew. Such soups, made in one pot, are everyday food. The addition of wine is not traditional, but enhances the richness of the broth.

INGREDIENTS

Serves 4
450g/1lb stewing beef, cubed
1.2 litres/2 pints/5 cups beef stock
300ml/½ pint/1¼ cups white wine
15ml/1 tbsp soft brown sugar
1 onion, finely chopped
1 bay leaf
1 bouquet garni
1 thyme sprig
15ml/1 tbsp tomato purée
1 large carrot, sliced
275g/10oz cassava or yam, cubed
50g/2oz fresh spinach, chopped
a little hot pepper sauce, to taste
salt and freshly ground black pepper

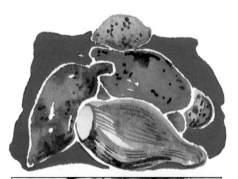

- COOK'S TIP -

If you like, a cheap cut of lamb can be used instead of beef and any other root vegetable can be used instead of, or as well as, the cassava or yam. Noodles, pasta shapes, or macaroni can also be used as a base, in which case cut down on the root vegetables in this broth. Omit the wine, if preferred, and add more water.

1 Put the beef, stock, wine, sugar, onion, bay leaf, bouquet garni, thyme and tomato purée in a large saucepan, bring to the boil and then cover and simmer for about 1¼ hours.

2 Add the carrot, cassava or yam, spinach, a few drops of hot pepper sauce, salt and pepper and simmer for a further 15 minutes until both the meat and vegetables are tender.

Fish and Sweet Potato Soup

The subtle sweetness of the potato combined with the fish and the aromatic flavour of oregano, makes this an appetizing soup.

INGREDIENTS

Serves 4
½ onion, chopped
175g/6oz sweet potato, peeled and diced
175g/6oz boneless white fish fillet, skinned
50g/2oz carrot, chopped
5ml/1 tsp fresh chopped oregano or 2.5ml/½ tsp dried
2.5ml/½ tsp ground cinnamon
1.35 litres/2¼ pints/5½ cups fish stock
75ml/5 tbsp single cream
chopped fresh parsley, to garnish

1 Put the onion, sweet potato, fish, carrot, oregano, cinnamon and half of the stock in a saucepan. Bring to the boil, then simmer for 20 minutes or until the potatoes are cooked.

2 Leave the liquid to cool, then pour into a blender or food processor and blend until smooth.

3 Return the soup to the saucepan, then add the remaining stock or water and gently bring to the boil. Reduce the heat to low and add the single cream, then gently heat through without boiling. Serve hot, garnished with the chopped parsley.

Caribbean Vegetable Soup

This vegetable soup is refreshing and filling and good as a main course for lunch. Cooked meat and fish can also be added.

INGREDIENTS

Serves 4
25g/1oz/2 tbsp butter or margarine
1 onion, chopped
1 garlic clove, crushed
2 carrots, sliced
1.5 litres/2½ pints/6¼ cups vegetable stock
2 bay leaves
2 thyme sprigs
1 celery stick, finely chopped
2 green bananas, peeled and cut into 4
175g/6oz white yam or eddoe, peeled and cubed
25g/1oz/2 tbsp red lentils
1 christophene, peeled and chopped
25g/1oz/2 tbsp macaroni (optional)
salt and freshly ground black pepper
chopped spring onion, to garnish

1 Melt the butter or margarine and fry the onion, garlic and carrots for a few minutes, stirring occasionally. Add the stock, bay leaves and thyme and bring to the boil.

2 Add the celery, green bananas, white yam or eddoe, lentils, christophene and macaroni, if using. Season and simmer for 25 minutes or until the vegetables are cooked. Serve garnished with spring onions.

COOK'S TIP

Use other root vegetables or potatoes if yam or eddoes are not available. Add more stock for a thinner soup.

Split Pea and Pumpkin Soup

Salt beef is often used in this creamy pea soup.

INGREDIENTS

Serves 4

225g/8oz split peas, soaked
1.2 litres/2 pints/5 cups water
25g/1oz/2 tbsp butter or margarine
1 onion, finely chopped
225g/8oz pumpkin, chopped
3 fresh tomatoes, peeled and chopped
5ml/1 tsp dried tarragon, crushed
15ml/1 tbsp chopped fresh coriander
2.5ml/½ tsp ground cumin
vegetable stock cube, crumbled
chilli powder, to taste
coriander sprigs, to garnish

1 Soak the split peas overnight in enough water to cover, then drain. Place the split peas in a large saucepan, add the water and boil for about 30 minutes until cooked.

2 In a separate pan, melt the butter or margarine and sauté the onion for a few minutes until soft but not browned.

3 Add the pumpkin, tomatoes, tarragon, coriander, cumin, vegetable stock cube and chilli powder and bring to the boil.

4 Stir the vegetable mixture into the cooked split peas and their liquid. Simmer gently for 20 minutes or until the vegetables are tender. If the soup is too thick, add another 150ml/¼ pint/⅔ cup of water. Serve hot, garnished with coriander.

Lamb and Lentil Soup

You could add more vegetables for a "bigger" soup.

INGREDIENTS

Serves 4

1.5 litres/2½ pints/6¼ cups water or
   stock
900g/2lb neck of lamb, cut into chops
½ onion, chopped
1 garlic clove, crushed
1 bay leaf
1 clove
2 thyme sprigs
225g/8oz potatoes
175g/6oz red lentils
600ml/1 pint/2½ cups water
salt and freshly ground black pepper
parsley, to garnish

1 Put the water and meat in a large
saucepan with the onion, garlic,
bay leaf, clove and thyme sprigs. Bring
to the boil and simmer for about
1 hour, until the lamb is tender.

2 Cut the potatoes into 2.5cm/1in
pieces and add to the pan.

3 Add the lentils to the pan and
season the soup with a little salt and
plenty of black pepper.

4 Add 300ml/½ pint/1¼ cups water
or more if the soup becomes too
thick, to come just above surface of the
meat and vegetables. Cover and
simmer for 25 minutes or until the
lentils are cooked and well blended
into the soup. Just before serving,
sprinkle in the parsley and stir well.

Spinach Patties

INGREDIENTS

Makes 10–12

For the pastry

250g/8oz/2 cups plain flour
115g/4oz/½ cup butter or margarine,
    chilled and diced
1 egg yolk
milk, to glaze

For the filling

25g/1oz/2 tbsp butter or margarine
1 small onion, finely chopped
175g–225g/6–8oz fresh or frozen leaf
    spinach, chopped
2.5ml/½ tsp ground cumin
½ vegetable stock cube, crumbled
freshly ground black pepper

1 Preheat the oven to 200°C/400°F/
Gas 6. Lightly grease the hollows of
a muffin or patty tin.

2 First make the spinach filling. Melt
the butter or margarine in a
saucepan, add the onion and cook
gently until softened. Stir in the spinach,
then add the cumin, stock cube and
pepper and cook for 5 minutes or until
the spinach has wilted. Leave to cool.

3 To make the pastry, put the flour
in a large bowl and rub in the
butter or margarine, until the mixture
resembles fine breadcrumbs. Add the
egg yolk and 30–45ml/2–3 tbsp cold
water and mix to a firm dough. Turn
out the pastry on to a floured surface.

4 Knead for a few seconds, divide the
dough in half and roll out one half to
a square or rectangle. Cut out 10–12
rounds using a 9cm/3½in pastry cutter.
Press into the hollows of the prepared
tin. Spoon about 15ml/1 tbsp of the
spinach mixture into the pastry cases.

5 Roll out the remaining dough and
cut out slightly smaller rounds to
cover the patties. Press the edges with a
fork, to seal. Prick the tops with the
fork. Brush with milk and bake for
15–20 minutes until golden brown.
Serve hot or cold.

Saltfish Fritters (Stamp and Go)

These delicious fritters are also
known as Accras.

INGREDIENTS

Makes 15

115g/4oz/1 cup self-raising flour
115g/4oz/1 cup plain flour
2.5ml/½ tsp baking powder
175g/6oz soaked salt cod, shredded
1 egg, whisked
15ml/1 tbsp chopped spring onion
1 garlic clove, crushed
2.5ml/½ tsp freshly ground black
    pepper
½ hot chilli pepper, seeded and finely
    chopped
1.5ml/¼ tsp turmeric
45ml/3 tbsp milk
vegetable oil, for shallow frying

1 Sift the flours and baking powder
together into a bowl, then add the
salt cod, egg, spring onion, garlic,
pepper, hot pepper and turmeric. Add
a little of the milk and mix well.

2 Gradually stir in the remaining
milk, adding just enough to make
a thick batter. Stir thoroughly so that all
ingredients are completely combined.

3 Heat a little oil in a large frying pan
until very hot. Add spoonfuls of
the mixture and fry for a few minutes
on each side until golden brown and
puffy. Lift out the fritters, drain on
kitchen paper and keep warm while
cooking the rest of the mixture in the
same way. Serve the fritters hot or
cold, as a snack.

Cheesy Eggs

Ideal as a snack for a cocktail party or as a starter. A variety of fillings can be used instead of cheese, such as sardines or tuna.

INGREDIENTS

Serves 4–6

6 eggs
15ml/1 tbsp mayonnaise
30ml/2 tbsp grated Cheddar cheese
2.5ml/½ tsp white pepper
10ml/2 tsp snipped fresh chives
2 radishes, thinly sliced, to garnish

1 Cook the eggs for about 10 minutes until hard-boiled. Leave the eggs to cool in cold water, then remove the shells.

2 Cut the eggs in half and place the egg yolks in a small bowl with the mayonnaise, cheese, pepper and chives.

3 Mash together with a fork until well blended.

4 Fill the whites with the egg and cheese mixture, and garnish with thinly sliced radishes.

Crab Cakes

These are quite delicious and they're just as good made with canned tuna fish, too.

INGREDIENTS

Makes about 15
225g/8oz white crab meat
115g/4oz cooked potatoes, mashed
25g/1oz/2 tbsp fresh herb seasoning
2.5ml/½ tsp mild mustard
2.5ml/½ tsp freshly ground black
    pepper
½ hot chilli pepper
15ml/1 tbsp shrimp paste (optional)
2.5ml/½ tsp dried oregano, crushed
1 egg, beaten
flour, for dusting
oil, for frying
lime wedges and basil leaves, to garnish

For the tomato dip
15ml/1 tbsp butter or margarine
½ onion, finely chopped
2 canned plum tomatoes, chopped
1 garlic clove, crushed
150ml/¼ pint/⅔ cup water
5–10ml/1–2 tsp malt vinegar
15ml/1 tbsp chopped fresh coriander
½ hot chilli pepper, chopped

1 To make the crab cakes, mix together the crab meat, potatoes, herb seasoning, mustard, peppers, shrimp paste, if using, oregano and egg in a large bowl. Chill for 30 minutes.

2 Make the tomato dip. Melt the butter or margarine in a small pan.

3 Add the onion, tomato and garlic and sauté for about 5 minutes until the onion is soft. Add the water, vinegar, coriander and hot pepper. Simmer for 10 minutes and then blend to a smooth purée in a food processor or blender and pour into a bowl. Keep warm or chill as required.

4 Using a spoon, shape the mixture into rounds and dust with flour. Heat a little oil in a frying pan and fry the crab cakes a few at a time for 2–3 minutes on each side until golden brown. Drain and keep warm while cooking the remaining cakes. Serve with the warm or cold tomato dip and garnish with lime wedges and basil leaves.

Plantain and Sweet Potato Crisps

INGREDIENTS

Serves 4
2 green plantains
1 small sweet potato
oil, for deep-frying
salt

1 Using a small sharp knife, top and tail the plantains and cut in half. Make three or four slits lengthways along the natural ridge of the plantains and lift away the skin. Place the plantains in a bowl of cold salted water.

2 Peel the sweet potato under cold running water, and add to the bowl of salted water.

3 Heat the oil in a large saucepan or deep-fat fryer. While the oil is heating, remove the vegetables one at a time from the salted water, pat dry on kitchen paper and slice into thin rounds with a sharp knife or vegetable slicer.

VARIATION

For maximum crispness, only green plantains should be used. If these are not available, green bananas can be used instead and yam is a good substitute for sweet potatoes. All of the vegetables should be soaked in cold salted water to prevent discoloration.

4 Fry the plantains and sweet potatoes until crisp, then drain and transfer to a dish lined with kitchen paper. Sprinkle with salt and cool.

Coconut King Prawns

INGREDIENTS

Serves 3–4
12 large raw prawns
2 garlic cloves, crushed
15ml/1 tbsp lemon juice
50g/2oz/4 tbsp fine desiccated coconut
25g/1oz/2 tbsp snipped fresh chives
150ml/¼ pint/⅔ cup milk
2 eggs, beaten
salt and freshly ground black pepper
oil, for deep frying
lime or lemon slices or wedges and flat-leaf parsley, to garnish

---

COOK'S TIP

If large raw prawns are difficult to obtain, substitute cooked prawns. However, the raw prawns will absorb more flavour from the marinade, so they are the ideal choice.

1 Peel and devein the prawns, leaving the tails intact, then cut the prawns along the length of their backs without cutting right through and fan them out. Rinse under cold water and pat dry.

2 Blend together the garlic, lemon juice and seasoning in a shallow dish, then add the prawns and marinate for about 1 hour.

3 Mix together the coconut and chives in a shallow dish, and put the milk and eggs in two separate dishes. Dip each prawn into the milk, then into the beaten egg and finally into the coconut and chive mixture.

4 Heat the oil in a large saucepan or deep-fat fryer and fry the prawns for about 1 minute, until golden. Drain on kitchen paper and serve hot garnished with the lime or lemon slices and parsley.

VEGETARIAN
DISHES
AND SALADS

Vegetarians will find they are spoilt for choice in the Caribbean and all cooks will enjoy the creative scope that the choice of vegetables and pulses provide. Tropical vegetables are usually available here all year round in this country although you may need to shop around and they will not be as plentiful or as inexpensive as in the Caribbean. Some of the recipes in this section are my version of well-loved international dishes which are also cooked in the Caribbean, such as Chow Mein, Red Bean Chilli and Macaroni Cheese Pie.

Spicy Potato Salad

This tasty salad is quick to prepare, and makes a satisfying accompaniment to grilled or barbecued meat or fish.

INGREDIENTS

Serves 6

900g/2lb potatoes, peeled
2 red peppers
2 celery sticks
1 shallot
2 or 3 spring onions
1 green chilli, finely chopped
1 garlic clove, crushed
10ml/2 tsp finely snipped
    fresh chives
10ml/2 tsp finely chopped fresh basil
15ml/1 tbsp finely chopped fresh
    parsley
15ml/1 tbsp single cream
30ml/2 tbsp salad cream
15ml/1 tbsp mayonnaise
5ml/1 tsp mild mustard
7.5ml/½ tbsp sugar
snipped fresh chives, to garnish

1 Boil the potatoes until tender but still firm. Drain and cool, then cut into 2.5cm/1in cubes and place in a large salad bowl.

2 Halve the peppers, cut away and discard the core and seeds and cut into small pieces. Finely chop the celery, shallot, and spring onions and slice the chilli very thinly, discarding the seeds. Add the vegetables to the potatoes together with the garlic and chopped herbs.

3 Blend the cream, salad cream, mayonnaise, mustard and sugar in a small bowl, stirring until the mixture is well combined.

4 Pour the dressing over the potato and vegetable salad and stir gently to coat evenly. Serve, garnished with the snipped chives.

Mango, Tomato and Red Onion Salad

This salad makes an appetizing starter, the under-ripe mango has a subtle sweetness and the flavour blends well with the tomato.

INGREDIENTS

Serves 4

1 firm under-ripe mango
2 large tomatoes or 1 beefsteak tomato, sliced
½ red onion, sliced into rings
½ cucumber, peeled and thinly sliced
30ml/2 tbsp sunflower or vegetable oil
15ml/1 tbsp lemon juice
1 garlic clove, crushed
2.5ml/½ tsp hot pepper sauce
salt and freshly ground black pepper
sugar, to taste
snipped chives, to garnish

1 Cut away two thick slices either side of the mango stone and cut into slices. Peel the skin from the slices.

2 Arrange the mango, tomato, onion and cucumber slices on a large serving plate.

3 Blend the oil, lemon juice, garlic, hot pepper sauce, salt and black pepper in a blender or food processor, or place in a small jar and shake vigorously. Add a pinch of sugar to taste and mix again.

4 Pour the dressing over the salad and garnish with snipped chives.

Spinach Plantain Rounds

This delectable way of serving plantains is a little fiddly to make, but well worth it! The plantains must be ripe, but still firm.

INGREDIENTS

Serves 4
2 large ripe plantains
oil, for frying
30ml/2 tbsp butter or margarine
25g/1oz/2 tbsp finely chopped onion
2 garlic cloves, crushed
450g/1lb fresh spinach, chopped
pinch of freshly grated nutmeg
1 egg, beaten
wholemeal flour, for dusting
salt and freshly ground black pepper

1 Using a small sharp knife, carefully cut each plantain lengthways into four slices.

2 Heat a little oil in a large frying pan and fry the plantain slices on both sides until lightly golden brown but not fully cooked. Drain on kitchen paper and reserve the oil.

3 Melt the butter or margarine in a saucepan and sauté the onion and garlic for a few minutes until the onion is soft. Add the spinach, salt, pepper and nutmeg. Cover and cook for about 5 minutes until the spinach has reduced. Cool, then tip into a sieve and press out any excess moisture.

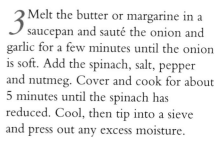

4 Curl the plantain slices into rings and secure each ring with a wooden cocktail stick. Pack each ring with a little of the spinach mixture.

5 Place the egg and flour in two separate shallow dishes. Add a little more oil to the frying pan if necessary and heat until moderately hot. Dip the plantain rings in the egg and then in the flour and fry on both sides for 1–2 minutes until golden brown. Drain on kitchen paper and serve hot or cold with a salad, or as part of a meal.

COOK'S TIP

If fresh spinach is not available, use frozen spinach, thawed and drained. The plantain rings can be small or large, and if preferred mashed meat, fish or beans can be used instead of spinach for the filling.

Peppery Bean Salad

This pretty salad uses canned beans for speed and convenience.

INGREDIENTS

Serves 4–6

425g/15oz can kidney beans, drained
425g/15oz can black-eyed beans, drained
425g/15oz can chick-peas, drained
¼ red pepper
¼ green pepper
6 radishes
15ml/1 tbsp chopped spring onion
5ml/1 tsp ground cumin
15ml/1 tbsp tomato ketchup
30ml/2 tbsp olive oil
15ml/1 tbsp white wine vinegar
1 garlic clove, crushed
½ tsp hot pepper sauce
salt
sliced spring onion, to garnish

1 Drain the canned beans and chick-peas and rinse under cold running water. Shake off the excess water and tip them into a large salad bowl.

2 Core, seed and chop the peppers. Trim the radishes and slice thinly. Add to the beans with the pepper and spring onion.

3 Mix together the cumin, ketchup, oil, vinegar and garlic in a small bowl. Add a little salt and hot pepper sauce to taste and stir again thoroughly.

4 Pour the dressing over the salad and mix. Chill for at least 1 hour before serving, garnished with spring onion.

COOK'S TIP

For an even tastier salad, allow the ingredients to marinate for a few hours.

Pigeon Peas, Christophene and Pumpkin Stew

INGREDIENTS

Serves 2–3

25g/1oz/2 tbsp butter or margarine
1 onion, chopped
2 garlic cloves, crushed
2 carrots, sliced
115g/4oz seeded, peeled pumpkin, chopped
1 christophene, peeled, stoned and chopped
115g/4oz pigeon peas
600ml/1 pint/2½ cups rich vegetable stock
2 thyme sprigs
15ml/1 tbsp fresh coriander leaves
25–50g/1–2oz creamed coconut
2.5ml/½ tsp ground cinnamon
hot pepper
salt
chopped fresh coriander, to garnish

1 Melt the butter or margarine in a large saucepan and sauté the onion and garlic for a few minutes until the onion is soft.

2 Stir in the carrots, pumpkin, christophene, pigeon peas, stock and thyme. Bring to the boil, then reduce the heat and simmer for 10 minutes.

3 Add the coriander, creamed coconut, cinnamon, hot pepper and salt. Simmer until the vegetables are tender and the sauce is reduced and thick. Serve hot, garnished with coriander.

> ──── Cook's Tip ────
>
> If christophene is not available, use courgettes or marrow instead. Canned beans or peas can be substituted for the pigeon peas.

Ackee with Mushrooms

Ackee is a fruit with a soft texture and a slight lemony flavour.

INGREDIENTS

Serves 4

25g/1oz/2 tbsp butter or margarine
30ml/2 tbsp vegetable oil
1 onion, chopped
2 garlic cloves, crushed
2 canned plum tomatoes plus 30ml/ 2 tbsp of the tomato juice
½ red pepper, chopped
1 hot chilli pepper, chopped (optional)
175g/6oz mushrooms, chopped
540g/1lb 6oz can ackee, drained
15ml/1 tbsp chopped fresh parsley
150ml/¼ pint/⅔ cup vegetable stock
salt
chopped fresh parsley and coriander sprigs, to garnish

1 Heat the butter or margarine and oil in a large frying pan, add the onion and garlic and sauté for a few minutes over a moderate heat until the onion has softened.

2 Add the canned tomatoes, tomato juice, red pepper, hot chilli pepper if using, mushrooms, ackee, parsley and season with salt to taste.

3 Stir gently, pour in the stock and slowly bring to the boil. Reduce the heat and simmer for 5 minutes. Serve with rice or boiled green bananas. Garnish with parsley and coriander.

> ──── Cook's Tip ────
>
> Use a metal spoon or fork and carefully mix, as ackee breaks up easily. Ackee adds a subtle flavour to most vegetables, beans or peas.

Macaroni Cheese Pie

INGREDIENTS

Serves 4

225g/8oz macaroni
25g/1oz/2 tbsp butter or margarine
45ml/3 tbsp plain flour
450ml/¾ pint/2 cups milk
5ml/1 tsp mild mustard
2.5ml/½ tsp ground cinnamon
175g/6oz mature Cheddar cheese,
    grated
1 egg, beaten
15ml/1 tbsp butter or margarine
25g/1oz/2 tbsp chopped spring onions
40g/1½oz/3 tbsp canned chopped
    tomatoes
115g/4oz/⅔ cup sweetcorn
freshly ground black pepper
chopped fresh parsley, to garnish

1 Heat the oven to 180°C/350°F/ Gas 4. Cook the macaroni in boiling salted water for 10 minutes until just tender. Rinse under cold water and drain.

2 Melt the butter or margarine in a saucepan and stir in the flour to make a roux. Slowly pour in the milk, whisking constantly, and simmer gently for 5–10 minutes.

3 Add the mustard, cinnamon and 115g/4oz of the cheese and cook gently, stirring frequently, then remove from the heat and whisk in the egg. Set aside and make the filling.

4 To make the filling, heat the butter or margarine in a small frying pan and cook the spring onions, chopped plum tomatoes and sweetcorn over a gentle heat for 5–10 minutes.

5 Tip half the cooked macaroni into a greased ovenproof dish. Pour over half the cheese sauce and mix well, then spoon the tomato and sweetcorn mixture over the macaroni.

6 Tip the remaining macaroni into the saucepan with the remaining sauce, stir well and then spread carefully over the tomato and sweetcorn mixture.

7 Top with the remaining grated cheese and bake in the oven for about 45 minutes, or until the top is golden and bubbly. If possible leave to stand for 30 minutes before serving. Serve hot, garnished with the chopped fresh parsley.

Red Bean Chilli

This vegetarian chilli can be adapted to accommodate meat eaters by adding either minced beef or lamb in place of the lentils. Add the meat once the onions are soft and fry until nicely browned before adding the tomatoes.

INGREDIENTS

Serves 4

30ml/2 tbsp vegetable oil
1 onion, chopped
400g/14oz can chopped tomatoes
2 garlic cloves, crushed
300ml/½ pint/1¼ cups white wine
about 300ml/½ pint/1¼ cups
    vegetable stock
115g/4oz red lentils
2 thyme sprigs or 5ml/1 tsp dried
    thyme
10ml/2 tsp ground cumin
45ml/3 tbsp dark soy sauce
½ hot chilli pepper, finely chopped
5ml/1 tsp mixed spice
15ml/1 tbsp oyster sauce (optional)
225g/8oz can red kidney beans,
    drained
10ml/2 tsp sugar
salt

1 Heat the oil in a large saucepan and fry the onion over a moderate heat for a few minutes until slightly softened.

2 Add the tomatoes and garlic, cook for 10 minutes, then stir in the wine and stock.

3 Add the lentils, thyme, cumin, soy sauce, hot pepper, mixed spice and oyster sauce, if using.

4 Cover and simmer for 40 minutes or until the lentils are cooked, stirring occasionally and adding more water if the lentils begin to dry out.

5 Stir in the kidney beans and sugar and continue cooking for 10 minutes, adding a little extra stock or water if necessary. Season to taste with salt and serve hot with boiled rice and sweetcorn.

—————— COOK'S TIP ——————

Fiery chillies can irritate the skin, so always wash your hands well after handling them and take care not to touch your eyes. If you like really hot, spicy food, then add the seeds from the chilli, too.

Spicy Vegetable Chow Mein

Chow mein is popular in Guyana, where it is usually made with shredded chicken or prawns. This vegetarian version can be adapted to suit all tastes.

INGREDIENTS

Serves 3
225g/8oz egg noodles
30–45ml/2–3 tbsp vegetable oil
2 garlic cloves, crushed
1 onion, chopped
115g/4oz each red and green pepper, chopped
115g/4oz French beans, blanched
40g/1½ oz/3 tbsp finely chopped celery
2.5ml/½ tsp five-spice powder
1 vegetable stock cube, crumbled
2.5ml/½ tsp freshly ground black pepper
15ml/1 tbsp soy sauce (optional)
salt

1 Cook the noodles in plenty of boiling salted water for 10 minutes or according to the packet instructions, then drain and spread out to cool, on a large plate.

2 Heat the oil in a wok or large frying pan and stir-fry the garlic, onion, red and green peppers, French beans and celery, tossing them together to mix.

3 Add the five-spice powder, the stock cube and black pepper, stir well and cook for 5 minutes.

4 Stir in the noodles and soy sauce, if using and season with salt. Serve.

─── COOK'S TIP ───

Shredded omelette or sliced hard-boiled eggs are also popular garnishes, and tuna fish chow mein is a children's favourite.

Aubergines Stuffed with Sweet Potato

INGREDIENTS

Serves 3–4
225g/8oz sweet potatoes, peeled
2.5ml/½ tsp chopped fresh thyme
75g/3oz Cheddar cheese, diced
25g/1oz/2 tbsp chopped spring onion
15ml/1 tbsp each chopped red and green pepper
1 garlic clove, crushed
2 large aubergines
30ml/2 tbsp plain flour
15ml/1 tbsp spice seasoning
olive oil, for frying
2 tomatoes, sliced
salt and freshly ground black pepper
chopped fresh parsley, to garnish

1 Preheat the oven to 180°C/350°F/ Gas 4. Cook the sweet potatoes until tender, then drain, place in a bowl and mash.

2 Add the thyme, cheese, spring onion, red and green peppers, garlic and salt and pepper and mix.

3 Cut each aubergine lengthways into four slices. Mix the flour and spice seasoning on a plate and dust over each aubergine slice.

4 Heat a little oil in a frying pan and fry the aubergine until browned, but not fully cooked. Drain and cool. Spoon a little of the potato mixture into the middle of each aubergine slice and roll up.

5 Butter two large pieces of foil and place four rolls on each. Add slices of tomato, wrap up the parcels and bake for 20 minutes. Serve hot, garnished with parsley.

FISH
AND
SEAFOOD

With its thousands of miles of shoreline, it's not surprising that fish plays an important part in Caribbean cookery. The recipes collected here include several traditional dishes, like Ackee and Saltfish, and Eschovished Fish, as well as others I've created myself which have a more contemporary flavour. In Caribbean recipes fish is always seasoned with herbs and spices and is either marinated, cooked or served with fresh lime juice or lemon juice. If fresh tropical fish is not available, then look out for frozen fish, available in many large supermarkets and Caribbean shops.

Creole Fish Stew

A simple attractive dish – good for a dinner party.

INGREDIENTS

Serves 4–6

2 whole red bream or large snapper, prepared and cut into 2.5cm/1in pieces
30ml/2 tbsp spice seasoning
30ml/2 tbsp malt vinegar
flour, for dusting
oil, for frying

For the sauce

30ml/2 tbsp vegetable oil
15ml/1 tbsp butter or margarine
1 onion, finely chopped
275g/10oz fresh tomatoes, peeled and finely chopped
2 garlic cloves, crushed
2 thyme sprigs
600ml/1 pint/2½ cups fish stock or water
2.5ml/½ tsp ground cinnamon
1 hot chilli pepper, chopped
115g/4oz each red and green pepper, finely chopped
salt
oregano sprigs, to garnish

1 Sprinkle the fish with the spice seasoning and vinegar, turning to coat. Set aside to marinate for at least 2 hours or overnight in the fridge.

2 When ready to cook, place a little flour on a large plate and coat the fish pieces, shaking off any excess flour.

3 Heat a little oil in a large frying pan and fry the fish pieces for about 5 minutes until golden brown, then set aside. Don't worry if the fish is not cooked through, it will finish cooking in the sauce.

4 To make the sauce, heat the oil and butter or margarine in a large frying pan or wok and stir-fry the onion for 5 minutes. Add the tomatoes, garlic and thyme, stir well and simmer for a further 5 minutes. Stir in the stock or water, cinnamon and hot pepper.

5 Add the fish pieces and the chopped peppers. Simmer until the fish is cooked through, and the stock has reduced to a thick sauce. Adjust the seasoning with salt. Serve hot, garnished with oregano.

Ackee and Saltfish

This is a classic of Jamaican cuisine, popular in the Caribbean served with boiled green bananas.

INGREDIENTS

Serves 4
450g/1lb salt cod
25g/1oz/2 tbsp butter or margarine
30ml/2 tbsp vegetable oil
1 onion, chopped
2 garlic cloves, crushed
225g/8oz chopped fresh tomatoes
½ hot chilli pepper, chopped (optional)
2.5ml/½ tsp freshly ground black pepper
2.5ml/½ tsp dried thyme
2.5ml/½ tsp ground allspice
30ml/2 tbsp chopped spring onion
540g/1lb 6oz can ackee, drained
Fried Dumplins, to serve

1 Place the salt cod in a bowl and cover with cold water. Leave it to soak for at least 12 hours, changing the water two or three times. Discard the water and rinse in fresh cold water.

2 Put the salt cod in a large saucepan of cold water, bring to the boil, then remove the fish and allow to cool on a plate. Remove and discard the skin and bones, then flake the fish and set aside.

3 Heat the butter or margarine and oil in a large heavy frying pan over a moderate heat. Add the onion and garlic and sauté for 5 minutes. Add the tomatoes and hot chilli pepper, if using, and cook gently for a further 5 minutes.

4 Add the salt cod, black pepper, thyme, allspice and spring onions, stir to mix then stir in the ackee, taking care not to crush them. If you prefer a moister dish, add a little water or stock. Serve hot with Fried Dumplins.

Salmon in Mango and Ginger Sauce

Mango and salmon complement each other, especially with the subtle flavour of tarragon.

INGREDIENTS

Serves 2
2 salmon steaks (about 275g/10oz each)
a little lemon juice
1 or 2 garlic cloves, crushed
5ml/1 tsp dried tarragon, crushed
2 shallots, roughly chopped
1 tomato, roughly chopped
1 ripe mango (about 175g/6oz flesh), chopped
150ml/¼ pint/⅔ cup fish stock or water
15ml/1 tbsp ginger syrup
25g/1oz/2 tbsp butter
salt and freshly ground black pepper

1 Place the salmon steaks in a shallow dish and season with the lemon juice, garlic, tarragon and salt and pepper. Set aside in the fridge to marinate for at least 1 hour.

2 Meanwhile, place the shallots, tomato and mango in a blender or food processor and blend until smooth. Add the fish stock or water and the ginger syrup, blend again and set aside.

3 Melt the butter in a frying pan and sauté the salmon steaks for about 5 minutes on each side.

4 Add the mango purée, cover and simmer until salmon is cooked.

5 Transfer the salmon to warmed serving plates. Heat the sauce through, adjust the seasoning and pour over the salmon. Serve hot.

Fried Snapper with Avocado

Caribbean fried fish is often eaten with fried dumplins or hard-dough bread, and, as in this recipe, is sometimes accompanied by avocado – it makes a delicious light supper or lunch.

INGREDIENTS

Serves 4
1 lemon
4 red snappers, about 225g/8oz each, prepared
10ml/2 tsp spice seasoning
flour, for dusting
oil, for frying
2 avocados and sliced corn-on-the-cob, to serve
chopped fresh parsley and lime slices, to garnish

1 Squeeze the lemon juice both inside and outside the fish and sprinkle them all over with the spice seasoning. Set the fish aside in a shallow dish to marinate in a cool place for a few hours.

2 Lift the fish out of the dish and dust thoroughly with the flour, shaking off the excess.

3 Heat the oil in a non-stick pan over a moderate heat. Add the fish and fry for about 10 minutes on each side until browned and crispy.

4 Halve the avocados, remove the stones and cut in half again. Peel away the skin and cut the flesh into thin strips.

5 Place the fish on warmed serving plates with the avocado and corn slices. Serve hot, garnished with parsley and lime slices.

Fillets of Trout in Wine Sauce with Plantains

Tropical fish would add a distinctive flavour to this dish, but any filleted white fish can be cooked in this way.

Ingredients

Serves 4

4 trout fillets
spice seasoning, for dusting
25g/1oz/2 tbsp butter or margarine
1 or 2 garlic cloves
150ml/¼ pint/²⁄₃ cup white wine
150ml/¼ pint/²⁄₃ cup fish stock
10ml/2 tsp honey
15–30ml/1–2 tbsp chopped fresh
  parsley
1 yellow plantain
salt and freshly ground black pepper
oil, for frying

1 Season the trout fillets with the spice seasoning and marinate for 1 hour.

2 Melt the butter or margarine in a large frying pan and heat gently for 1 minute. Add the fillets and sauté for about 5 minutes, until cooked through, turning carefully once. Transfer to a plate and keep warm.

COOK'S TIP

Plantains belong to the banana family and can be green, yellow, or brown, depending on ripeness. Unlike bananas, plantains must be cooked. Their subtle flavour works well in spicy dishes.

3 Add the wine, fish stock and honey to the pan, bring to the boil and simmer to reduce slightly. Return the fillets to the pan and spoon over the sauce. Sprinkle with parsley and simmer gently for a few minutes.

4 Meanwhile, peel the plantain, and cut into rounds. Heat a little oil in a frying pan and fry the plantain slices for a few minutes, until golden, turning once. Transfer the fish to warmed serving plates, stir the sauce, adjust the seasoning and pour over the fish. Garnish with the fried plantain.

Eschovished Fish

This dish is of Spanish origin and is very popular throughout the Caribbean. There are as many variations of the name of the dish as there are ways of preparing it.

INGREDIENTS

Serves 4–6
900g/2lb cod fillet
½ lemon
15ml/1 tbsp spice seasoning
flour, for dusting
oil, for frying
lemon wedges, to garnish

For the sauce
30ml/2 tbsp vegetable oil
1 onion, sliced
½ red pepper, sliced
½ christophene, peeled and seeded, cut into small pieces
2 garlic cloves, crushed
120ml/4fl oz/½ cup malt vinegar
75ml/5 tbsp water
2.5ml/½ tsp ground allspice
1 bay leaf
1 small Scotch Bonnet pepper, chopped
15ml/1 tbsp soft brown sugar
salt and freshly ground black pepper

1 Place the fish in a shallow dish, squeeze over the lemon, then sprinkle with the spice seasoning and pat into the fish. Leave to marinate in a cool place for at least 1 hour.

2 Cut the fish into 7.5cm/3in pieces and dust with a little flour, shaking off the excess.

3 Heat the oil in a heavy frying pan and fry the fish pieces for 2–3 minutes until golden brown and crisp, turning occasionally. To make the sauce, heat the oil in a heavy frying pan and fry the onion until soft.

4 Add the pepper, christophene and garlic and stir-fry for 2 minutes. Pour in the vinegar, then add the remaining ingredients and simmer gently for 5 minutes. Leave to stand for 10 minutes, then pour over the fish. Serve hot, garnished with lemon wedges.

COOK'S TIP

In the Caribbean, whole red snapper or red mullet are used for this dish.

King Prawns in Sweetcorn Sauce

This sauce makes a hearty filling for baked sweet potatoes.

INGREDIENTS

Serves 4

24–30 large raw prawns
spice seasoning, for dusting
juice of 1 lemon
30ml/2 tbsp butter or margarine
1 onion, chopped
2 garlic cloves, crushed
30ml/2 tbsp tomato purée
2.5ml/½ tsp dried thyme
2.5ml/½ tsp ground cinnamon
15ml/1 tbsp chopped fresh coriander
½ hot chilli pepper, chopped
175g/6oz frozen or canned sweetcorn
300ml/½ pint/1¼ cups coconut milk
chopped fresh coriander, to garnish

1 Sprinkle the prawns with spice seasoning and lemon juice and marinate in a cool place for an hour.

2 Melt the butter or margarine in a saucepan, fry the onion and garlic for 5 minutes, until slightly softened. Add the prawns and cook for a few minutes, stirring occasionally until cooked through and pink.

3 Transfer the prawns, onion and garlic to a bowl, leaving behind some of the buttery liquid. Add the tomato purée to the pan and cook over a low heat, stirring thoroughly. Add the thyme, cinnamon, coriander and hot pepper and stir well.

4 Blend the sweetcorn (reserving 15ml/1 tbsp) in a blender or food processor with the coconut milk. Add to the pan and simmer until reduced. Add the prawns and reserved corn, and simmer for 5 minutes. Serve hot, garnished with coriander.

COOK'S TIP

If you use raw king prawns, make a stock from the shells and use in place of some of the coconut milk.

Prawns and Saltfish with Okra

An unusual mix of saltfish and prawns, enhanced by the okra.

INGREDIENTS

Serves 4

450g/1lb raw prawns, peeled
15ml/1 tbsp spice seasoning
25g/1oz/2 tbsp butter or margarine
15ml/1 tbsp olive oil
2 shallots, finely chopped
1 garlic clove, crushed
350g/12oz okra, topped, tailed and cut
    into 2.5cm/1in lengths
5ml/1 tsp curry powder
10ml/2 tsp shrimp paste
15ml/1 tbsp chopped fresh coriander
15ml/1 tbsp lemon juice
175g/6oz prepared saltfish (see Cook's
    Tip), shredded

1 Season the prawns with the spice seasoning and leave to marinate in a cool place for about 1 hour.

2 Heat the butter or margarine and olive oil in a large frying pan or wok over a moderate heat and stir-fry the shallots and garlic for 5 minutes. Add the okra, curry powder and shrimp paste, stir well and cook for about 10 minutes, until the okra is tender.

3 Add 30ml/2 tbsp water, coriander, lemon juice, prawns and saltfish, and cook gently for 5–10 minutes. Adjust the seasoning and serve hot.

COOK'S TIP

Soak the saltfish for 12 hours, changing the water two or three times. Rinse, bring to the boil in fresh water, then cool.

Crab and Corn Gumbo

INGREDIENTS

Serves 4

25g/1oz/2 tbsp butter or margarine
25g/1oz/2 tbsp plain flour
15ml/1 tbsp vegetable oil
1 onion, finely chopped
115g/4oz okra, trimmed and chopped
2 garlic cloves, crushed
15ml/1 tbsp finely chopped celery
600ml/1 pint/2½ cups fish stock
150ml/¼ pint/⅔ cup sherry
15ml/1 tbsp tomato ketchup
2.5ml/½ tsp dried oregano
1.5ml/¼ tsp mixed spice
10ml/2 tsp Worcestershire sauce
hot pepper
2 corn-on-the-cob, chopped
450g/1lb crab claws
fresh coriander, to garnish

1 Melt the butter or margarine in a large saucepan over a low heat, add the flour and stir together to make a roux. Cook for about 10 minutes, stirring constantly, to prevent burning, while the roux turns golden brown and then darkens. Turn the roux on to a plate and set aside.

2 Heat the oil in the same saucepan over a moderate heat, add the onion, okra, garlic and celery and stir to mix together. Cook for a few minutes, then add the stock, sherry, ketchup, oregano, mixed spice, Worcestershire sauce and hot pepper.

3 Bring to the boil, then simmer gently for about 10 minutes until the vegetables are tender. Add the roux, stirring it well into the sauce and cook for a few minutes until thickened.

4 Add the corn and crab claws and continue to simmer gently over a low heat for about 10 minutes until the crab and corn are cooked.

5 Spoon on to warmed serving plates and garnish with sprigs of fresh coriander.

Pumpkin and Prawns with Dried Shrimps

INGREDIENTS

Serves 4

50g/2oz dried shrimps
30ml/2 tbsp vegetable or
   sunflower oil
25g/1oz/2 tbsp butter or margarine
1 red onion, chopped
790g/1¾lb pumpkin, peeled
   and chopped
225g/8oz cooked, peeled prawns
2.5ml/½ tsp ground cinnamon
2.5ml/½ tsp five-spice powder
2 garlic cloves, chopped
2 fresh tomatoes, chopped
chopped fresh parsley and lime
   wedges, to garnish

1 Rinse the dried shrimps under cold water and then soak them, in enough hot water to cover, for 35 minutes.

2 Heat the oil and butter or margarine in a large frying pan over a moderate heat. Add the onion and sauté for 5 minutes until soft.

3 Add the pumpkin and cook for 5–6 minutes, until the pumpkin is slightly tender. Add the peeled prawns and the dried shrimps together with their soaking water. Stir in the cinnamon, five-spice powder and the chopped garlic.

4 Add the tomatoes and cook over a gentle heat, stirring occasionally, until the pumpkin is soft.

5 Spoon on to a warmed serving plate and serve hot, garnished with the chopped parsley.

MEAT AND POULTRY

Caribbean Mutton Curry, Barbecued Jerk Chicken, Pork Roasted with Herbs, Spices and Rum, and Spicy Fried Chicken are traditional favourites in the Caribbean and are eaten at festivals, celebrations and at big family get-togethers.

Along with these recipes, I've also included newly created recipes such as Thyme and Lime Chicken, and Peanut Chicken which are simple and quick, yet have an authentic Caribbean taste. Many meat dishes originate from Africa and the meat is cooked with vegetables and pulses, while the ever-popular chicken can be served in a variety of ways.

Hearty Beef Stew

The brown ale gives this beef stew a real kick. Vary the amount to suit your taste.

INGREDIENTS

Serves 4
50g/2oz black-eyed beans
25g/1oz/2 tbsp butter or margarine
1 onion, chopped
675g/1½lb stewing beef, cubed
5ml/1 tsp paprika
2 garlic cloves, crushed
10ml/2 tsp ground cinnamon
10ml/2 tsp sugar
600ml/1 pint/2½ cups beef stock
150ml/¼ pint/⅔ cup brown ale
45ml/3 tbsp evaporated milk
salt and freshly ground black pepper
baby patty-pan squash, to serve

1 Soak the black-eyed beans overnight, then place in a large saucepan, cover with water and bring to the boil. Boil rapidly for a few minutes then reduce the heat and simmer for about 30 minutes or until the beans are cooked and tender but still quite firm. Drain the beans, reserving the cooking liquid.

2 Meanwhile, melt the butter or margarine in a large saucepan and sauté the onion for a few minutes. Add the beef, paprika, garlic, cinnamon and sugar and fry for about 5 minutes until the beef is browned, stirring frequently.

3 Add the beef stock and brown ale, cover and cook for 45–60 minutes, until the beef is almost cooked.

4 Add the milk, beans and salt and pepper and continue cooking until the beans and beef are tender. Add a little of the reserved bean liquid, if the stew begins to dry out. Adjust the seasoning and serve with steamed baby patty-pan squash.

Caribbean Lamb Curry

This popular national dish of Jamaica is known as Curry Goat although goat meat or lamb can be used to make it.

INGREDIENTS

Serves 4–6

2 pounds boned leg of lamb
4 tablespoons curry powder
3 garlic cloves, crushed
1 large onion, chopped
4 thyme sprigs or 1 teaspoon dried thyme
3 bay leaves
1 teaspoon ground allspice
2 tablespoons vegetable oil
4 tablespoons butter or margarine
3¾ cups stock or water
1 fresh hot chili pepper, chopped
cooked rice, to serve
cilantro sprigs, to garnish

1 Cut the meat into 2-inch cubes, discarding any excess fat and gristle.

2 Place the lamb, curry powder, garlic, onion, thyme, bay leaves, allspice and oil in a large bowl and mix. Marinate in the fridge for at least 3 hours or overnight.

3 Melt the butter or margarine in a large heavy saucepan, add the seasoned lamb and fry over a moderate heat for about 10 minutes, turning the meat frequently.

4 Stir in the stock and chili pepper and bring to a boil. Reduce the heat, cover the pan and simmer for 1½ hours, or until the meat is tender. Serve with rice, garnish with cilantro.

COOK'S TIP

Try goat, or mutton, if you can and enjoy a robust curry.

Pork Roasted with Herbs, Spices and Rum

In the Caribbean, this spicy roast pork is usually barbecued and served on special occasions, as part of a buffet.

INGREDIENTS

Serves 6–8
2 garlic cloves, crushed
45ml/3 tbsp soy sauce
15ml/1 tbsp malt vinegar
15ml/1 tbsp finely chopped celery
30ml/2 tbsp chopped spring onion
7.5ml/1½ tsp dried thyme
5ml/1 tsp dried sage
2.5ml/½ tsp mixed spice
10ml/2 tsp curry powder
120ml/4fl oz/½ cup rum
15ml/1 tbsp demerara sugar
1.5kg/3–3.5lb joint of pork, boned and scored
salt and freshly ground black pepper
creamed sweet potato, to serve
spring onion curls, to garnish

For the sauce
25g/1oz/2 tbsp butter or margarine
15ml/1 tbsp tomato purée
300ml/½ pint/1¼ cups stock
15ml/1 tbsp chopped fresh parsley
15ml/1 tbsp demerara sugar
hot pepper sauce, to taste
salt

1 Mix together the garlic, soy sauce, vinegar, celery, spring onion, thyme, sage, mixed spice, curry powder, rum, demerara sugar and salt and pepper.

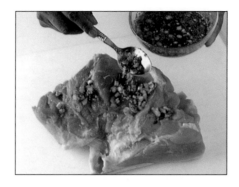

2 Open out the pork and slash the meat, without cutting through. Spread the mixture all over the pork, pressing it well into the slashes. Rub the outside of the joint with the mixture and refrigerate overnight.

3 Preheat the oven to 190°C/375°F/ Gas 5. Roll the meat up, then tie tightly in several places with strong cotton string to hold the meat together.

4 Spread a large piece of foil across a roasting tin and place the joint in the centre. Baste the pork with a few spoonfuls of the marinade and wrap the foil around the joint, holding in the marinade.

5 Bake in the oven for 1¾ hours, then remove the foil, baste with any remaining marinade and cook for a further 1 hour. Check occasionally that the joint is not drying out and baste with any pan juices.

6 Transfer the pork to a warmed serving dish and leave to stand in a warm place for 15 minutes before serving. Meanwhile make the sauce, pour the pan juices into a saucepan. Add the butter or margarine.

7 Add the tomato purée, stock, parsley, sugar, hot pepper and salt to taste. Simmer gently until reduced. Serve the pork sliced, with sweet potato. Garnish with spring onion curls and hand the sauce separately.

COOK'S TIP

In the Caribbean pork is baked until it is very well done, so reduce the cooking time to suit if you prefer meat slightly moister. To get the full flavour from the marinade, start to prepare the pork the night before you want to eat it.

Peppered Steak in Sherry Cream Sauce

This dish would be perfect for supper, served on a bed of noodles or with boiled plantains.

INGREDIENTS

Serves 4

675g/1½lb frying steak
5ml/1 tsp spice seasoning
25g/1oz/2 tbsp butter
6–8 shallots, sliced
2 garlic cloves, crushed
120ml/4fl oz/½ cup sherry
45ml/3 tbsp water
75ml/5 tbsp single cream
salt and freshly ground black pepper
cooked plantain, to serve
snipped fresh chives, to garnish

1 Cut the meat into thin strips, discarding any fat or gristle.

2 Season the meat with pepper and spice seasoning and leave to marinate in a cool place for 30 minutes.

3 Melt the butter in a large frying pan and sauté the meat for 4–5 minutes until browned on all sides. Transfer to a plate and set aside.

4 Add the shallots and garlic to the pan, fry gently for a few minutes then add the sherry and water and simmer for 5 minutes. Stir in the single cream.

5 Reduce the heat and adjust the seasoning. Stir in the meat and heat until hot but not boiling. Serve with plantain and garnish with chives.

Oxtail and Butter Beans

This is a traditional Caribbean stew; old-fashioned, economical and full of goodness. It requires patience because of the long cooking time and since there isn't much meat on the oxtail it's necessary to buy a large amount. Ask your butcher to chop the oxtail unless, of course, you can use a meat cleaver!

INGREDIENTS

Serves 4 or more

1.5kg/3lb oxtail, chopped into pieces
1.75 litres/3 pints/7½ cups water
1 onion, finely chopped
3 bay leaves
4 thyme sprigs
3 whole cloves
175g/6oz dried butter beans, soaked
   overnight
2 garlic cloves, crushed
15ml/1 tbsp tomato purée
400g/14oz can chopped tomatoes
5ml/1 tsp ground allspice
1 hot chilli pepper
salt and freshly ground black pepper

1 Place the oxtail in a large heavy pan, add the onion, bay leaves, thyme and cloves and cover with water. Bring to the boil, then reduce the heat.

2 Cover the pan and simmer for at least 2½ hours or until the meat is very tender, adding water whenever necessary.

3 Meanwhile, drain the beans and cover with water. Bring to the boil and simmer for 1–1¼ hours. Drain and set aside.

4 When the oxtail is cooked and the stock is well reduced, add the garlic, tomato purée, tomatoes, allspice, hot pepper, salt and black pepper. Add the butter beans and simmer for a further 20 minutes. The stew should be fairly thick, but if it looks dry add a little water. Adjust the seasoning and serve hot.

Pot Roast of Beef with Red Onions

The French-Caribbean culinary tradition of marinating and spicing meat has been used to create this warmly spiced pot roast with an oriental touch. Use a heavy-based pan – a cast-iron casserole is ideal – and simmer the beef over a very low heat until it is meltingly tender.

INGREDIENTS

Serves 6–8

1.5–1.7kg/3–4lb boned and rolled
   joint of beef, such as topside
   or silverside
15ml/1 tbsp hoi-sin sauce
2 garlic cloves, crushed
15ml/1 tbsp spice seasoning
1 red onion, thinly sliced
½ green pepper, thinly sliced
300ml/½ pint/1¼ cups red wine
300ml/½ pint/1¼ cups cold
   beef stock
fine cornmeal or plain flour,
   for dusting
30ml/2 tbsp vegetable oil
4 or 5 fresh basil leaves
basil sprigs, to garnish

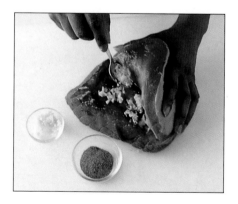

1 Untie the joint of beef and open out on a flat surface. Spread with the hoi-sin sauce, garlic and half the spice seasoning and then scatter half of the onion, pepper and a few of the basil leaves on top. Fold over the end of the joint, roll up and re-tie with strong cotton string. Sprinkle with the remaining spice seasoning.

2 Place the meat in a large bowl and add enough wine and cold beef stock to cover. Cover loosely with clear film and leave to marinate in the fridge for at least 8 hours or overnight.

3 Remove the meat, reserving the marinade. Roll the joint in the cornmeal. Heat the oil in a large saucepan and brown the meat on all sides.

4 Lift the meat out on to a plate and pour away excess oil. Return the meat to the pan and add the reserved marinade, onion, pepper and basil.

5 Bring to the boil, then cover and simmer gently for about 2½ hours, or until the beef is tender.

6 Transfer the meat to a warmed serving plate and boil the cooking liquid until it is slightly syrupy and reduced by about half. Pour into a serving jug and serve with the meat, accompanied with creamed sweet potatoes and okra, and garnished with basil.

--- VARIATIONS ---

If you can't find red onions, use shallots, which have a similar mild flavour, or simply substitute an ordinary onion. The beef can be roasted in a low oven, if you prefer. Instead of red wine, use the same quantity of stock or water.

"Seasoned-up" Lamb in Spinach Sauce

Lamb, spinach and ginger go well together. Powdered ginger has a strong distinctive flavour and should be used sparingly – you could use grated fresh root ginger, if you prefer.

INGREDIENTS

Serves 4
675g/1½lb stewing lamb, cubed
2.5ml/½ tsp ground ginger
2.5ml/½ tsp dried thyme
30ml/2 tbsp olive oil
1 onion, chopped
2 garlic cloves, crushed
15ml/1 tbsp tomato purée
½ hot chilli pepper chopped (optional)
600ml/1 pint/2½ cups stock or water
115g/4oz fresh spinach, finely chopped
salt and freshly ground black pepper

1 Place the lamb in a glass or china dish, season with the ginger, thyme and salt and pepper and leave to marinate in a cool place for at least 2 hours or overnight in the fridge.

2 Heat the olive oil in a large heavy saucepan, add the onion and garlic and fry gently for 5 minutes or until the onion is soft.

3 Add the lamb together with the tomato purée and hot pepper, if using. Fry over a moderate heat for about 5 minutes, stirring frequently, then add the stock or water. Cover and simmer for about 30 minutes, until the lamb is tender. Stir in the spinach. Simmer for 8 minutes until the sauce is fairly thick. Serve hot with boiled rice or root vegetables.

Lamb Pelau

Rice is often cooked with meat and coconut milk.

INGREDIENTS

Serves 4
450g/1lb stewing lamb
15ml/1 tbsp curry powder
1 onion, chopped
2 garlic cloves, crushed
2.5ml/½ tsp dried thyme
2.5ml/½ tsp dried oregano
1 fresh or dried chilli
25g/1oz/2 tbsp butter or margarine,
  plus more for serving
600ml/1 pint/2½ cups beef or chicken
  stock or coconut milk
5ml/1 tsp freshly ground black pepper
2 tomatoes, chopped
10ml/2 tsp sugar
30ml/2 tbsp chopped spring onion
450g/1lb basmati rice
spring onion strips, to garnish

1 Cut the lamb into cubes and place in a shallow glass or china dish. Sprinkle with the curry powder, onion, garlic, herbs and chilli and stir well. Cover loosely with clear film and leave to marinate in a cool place for 1 hour.

2 Melt the butter or margarine in a saucepan and fry the lamb for 5–10 minutes, on all sides. Add the stock or coconut milk, bring to the boil, then lower the heat and simmer for 35 minutes or until the meat is tender.

3 Add the black pepper, tomatoes, sugar, spring onions and rice, stir well and reduce the heat. Make sure that the rice is covered by 2.5cm/1in of liquid and add a little water if necessary. Simmer the pelau for 25 minutes or until the rice is cooked, then stir a little extra butter or margarine into the rice before serving. Garnish with spring onion strips.

Barbecued Jerk Chicken

Jerk refers to the blend of herb and spice seasoning rubbed into meat, before it is roasted over charcoal sprinkled with pimiento berries. In Jamaica, jerk seasoning was originally used only for pork, but jerked chicken is equally good.

INGREDIENTS

Serves 4
8 chicken pieces

For the marinade
5ml/1 tsp ground allspice
5ml/1 tsp ground cinnamon
5ml/1 tsp dried thyme
1.5ml/¼ tsp freshly grated nutmeg
10ml/2 tsp demerara sugar
2 garlic cloves, crushed
15ml/1 tbsp finely chopped onion
15ml/1 tbsp chopped spring onion
15ml/1 tbsp vinegar
30ml/2 tbsp oil
15ml/1 tbsp lime juice
1 hot chilli pepper, chopped
salt and freshly ground black pepper
salad leaves, to serve

1 Combine all the marinade ingredients in a small bowl. Using a fork, mash them together well to form a thick paste.

2 Lay the chicken pieces on a plate or board and make several lengthways slits in the flesh. Rub the seasoning all over the chicken and into the slits.

3 Place the chicken pieces in a dish, cover with clear film and marinate overnight in the fridge.

4 Shake off any excess seasoning from the chicken. Brush with oil and either place on a baking sheet or on a barbecue grill if barbecuing. Cook under a preheated grill for 45 minutes, turning often. Or, if barbecuing, light the coals and when ready, cook over the coals for 30 minutes, turning often. Serve hot with salad leaves.

COOK'S TIP

The flavour is best if you marinate the chicken overnight. Sprinkle the charcoal with aromatic herbs such as bay leaves for even more flavour.

Thyme and Lime Chicken

INGREDIENTS

Serves 4

8 chicken thighs
30ml/2 tbsp chopped spring onion
5ml/1 tsp dried or chopped fresh thyme
2 garlic cloves, crushed
juice of 1 lime or lemon
90ml/6 tbsp melted butter
salt and freshly ground black pepper
cooked rice, to serve
lime slices and coriander sprigs,
    to garnish

1 Put the chicken thighs in an ovenproof dish or on a baking tray skin-side down and using a sharp knife, make a slit, lengthways along the thigh bone of each thigh. Mix the spring onion with a little salt and pepper and press the mixture into the slits.

2 Mix together the thyme, garlic, lime or lemon juice and all but 30ml/2 tbsp of the butter in a small bowl and spoon a little over each chicken thigh.

3 Spoon the remaining butter over the top. Cover the chicken loosely with clear film and leave to marinate in a cool place for several hours or overnight in the fridge.

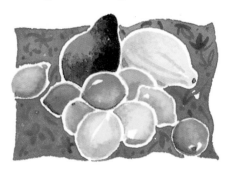

4 Preheat the oven to 190°C/375°F/ Gas 5. Remove the clear film from the chicken and cover the dish with foil. Bake the chicken for 1 hour, then remove the foil and cook for a few more minutes to brown. Serve hot, with rice and garnish with lime and coriander.

COOK'S TIP

You may need to use two limes, depending on their size and juiciness. Or, for a less sharp flavour, use lemons instead.

Spicy Fried Chicken

This crispy chicken is superb hot or cold. Served with a salad or vegetables, it makes a delicious lunch and is ideal for picnics or snacks too.

INGREDIENTS

Serves 4–6
4 chicken drumsticks
4 chicken thighs
10ml/2 tsp curry powder
2.5ml/½ tsp garlic granules
2.5ml/½ tsp ground black pepper
2.5ml/½ tsp paprika
about 300ml/½ pint/1¼ cups milk
oil, for deep frying
50g/2oz/4 tbsp plain flour
salt
salad leaves, to serve

1 Place the chicken pieces in a large bowl and sprinkle with the curry powder, garlic granules, black pepper, paprika and salt. Rub the spices well into the chicken, then cover and leave to marinate in a cool place for at least 2 hours, or overnight in the fridge.

2 Preheat the oven to 180°C/350°F/ Gas 4. Pour enough milk into the bowl to cover the chicken and leave to stand for a further 15 minutes.

3 Heat the oil in a large saucepan or deep-fat fryer and tip the flour on to a plate. Shake off excess milk, dip each piece of chicken in flour and fry two or three pieces at a time until golden, but not cooked. Continue until all the chicken pieces are fried.

4 Remove with a slotted spoon, place the chicken pieces on a baking tray, and bake for about 30 minutes. Serve hot or cold with salad.

Sunday Roast Chicken

INGREDIENTS

Serves 6

1.5kg/3–3½lb chicken
5ml/1 tsp paprika
5ml/1 tsp dried thyme
2.5ml/½ tsp dried tarragon
5ml/1 tsp garlic granules
15ml/1 tbsp lemon juice
30ml/2 tbsp honey
45ml/3 tbsp dark rum
melted butter, for basting
300ml/½ pint/1¼ cups chicken stock
lime quarters, to garnish

1 Place the chicken in a roasting tin and sprinkle with the paprika, thyme, tarragon, garlic granules and salt and pepper. Rub the mixture all over the chicken, lifting the skin and spreading the seasoning underneath it too. Cover the chicken loosely with clear film and leave to marinate in a cool place for at least 2 hours or preferably overnight in the fridge.

--- COOK'S TIP ---

Extra herbs and rum can be used to make a richer, tastier gravy, if you like.

2 Preheat the oven to 190°C/375°F/ Gas 5. Blend together the lemon juice, honey and rum and pour over and under the skin of the chicken rubbing it in well.

3 Spoon the melted butter all over the chicken, then transfer to the oven and roast for 1½–2 hours.

4 Pour the pan juices from the chicken into a small saucepan. Keep the chicken warm while you make the sauce. Add the chicken stock to the pan and simmer over a low heat for 10 minutes or until reduced. Adjust the seasoning and pour into a serving jug. Serve with the chicken and garnish with lime quarters.

Peanut Chicken

In this dish the rich nutty sauce is best made from smooth peanut butter, though it can also be made with crushed peanuts.

INGREDIENTS

Serves 4

900g/2lb chicken breasts, boned and
   skinned and cut into pieces.
2 garlic cloves, crushed
2.5ml/½ tsp dried thyme
2.5ml/½ tsp freshly ground black pepper
15ml/1 tbsp curry powder
15ml/1 tbsp lemon juice
25g/1oz/2 tbsp butter or margarine
1 onion, chopped
45ml/3 tbsp chopped tomatoes
1 hot chilli pepper, chopped
30ml/2 tbsp smooth peanut butter
450ml/¾ pint/1⅞ cups warm water
salt
fried plantain, to serve
coriander sprigs, to garnish

1 Place the chicken pieces into a large bowl and stir in the garlic, thyme, black pepper, curry powder, lemon juice and a little salt. Cover loosely with clear film and leave to marinate in a cool place for a few hours.

2 Melt the butter or margarine in a large saucepan, add the onion and sauté gently for 5 minutes, then add the seasoned chicken. Fry over a medium heat for 10 minutes, turning frequently and then add the tomatoes and the hot pepper and stir well.

3 Blend the peanut butter with a little of the warm water to a smooth paste and stir into the chicken mixture.

4 Slowly stir in the remaining water and simmer gently for about 30 minutes adding a little more water if necessary. Serve hot with fried plantain and garnish with coriander sprigs.

Breasts of Turkey with Mango and Wine

Fresh mango gives this dish a truly tropical taste.

INGREDIENTS

Serves 4

4 turkey breast fillets
1 garlic clove, crushed
1.5ml/¼ tsp ground cinnamon
15ml/1 tbsp finely chopped fresh
   parsley
15ml/1 tbsp crushed cream crackers
25g/1oz/2 tbsp chopped ripe mango
40g/1½oz/3 tbsp butter or margarine
1 garlic clove, crushed
6 shallots, sliced
150ml/¼ pint/⅔ cup white wine
salt and freshly ground black pepper
diced fresh mango and chopped fresh
   parsley, to garnish

1 Cut a slit horizontally through each turkey fillet to make a "pocket".

2 Put the garlic, cinnamon, parsley, cracker crumbs, mango, 15ml/ 1 tbsp of the butter or margarine and salt and pepper in a bowl and mash together. Spoon a little mixture into each of the "pockets" and if necessary secure with a wooden cocktail stick. Season with a little extra pepper.

3 Melt the remaining butter or margarine in a large frying pan and sauté the garlic and shallots for 5 minutes. Add the turkey fillets and cook for 15 minutes, turning once. Add the wine, cover and simmer gently, until the turkey is fully cooked. Add the diced mango, heat through for a minute or two and serve, garnished with the parsley.

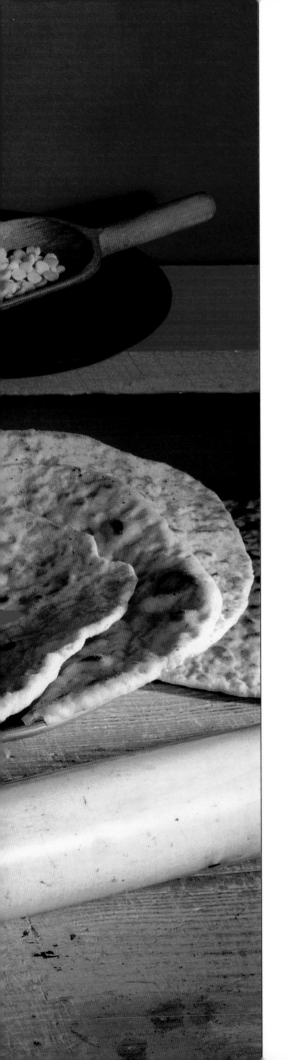

BREADS AND SIDE DISHES

Meat and fish dishes are never served alone in the Caribbean, but are always accompanied by side dishes. Almost all filling or carbohydrate-rich foods like rice, pulses, potatoes and bread are popular in the Caribbean, although rice, whether simply boiled, or cooked with peas or vegetables is most widely eaten. Peas and Rice is a traditional dish throughout the Caribbean, although variations do occur, such as in the Eastern Caribbean islands and Guyana, where pigeon peas take the place of red kidney beans. Some side dishes such as Aubergines with Garlic and Spring Onions are excellent by themselves, and can be served as a main meal with Rice and Peas, and salad.

Dhal Puri

Otherwise known as roti, these thin fried breads can also be made with white flour. They are delicious served with meat, fish or vegetable dishes.

Ingredients

Makes about 15
450g/1lb/4 cups self-raising flour
115g/4oz/1 cup wholemeal flour
350ml/12fl oz/1½ cups cold water
30ml/2 tbsp oil, plus extra for frying
salt, to taste

For the filling
350g/12oz yellow split peas
15ml/1 tbsp ground cumin
2 garlic cloves, crushed

1 Sift together the dry ingredients into a bowl, then add the water a little at a time gradually kneading the mixture to make a soft dough. Knead for a short while until supple.

2 Add the oil to the dough and continue to knead until completely smooth. Put the dough in a polythene bag or wrap in clear film and keep in a cool place or in the fridge for at least 30 minutes, or leave overnight.

3 To make the filling, put the peas in a saucepan, cover with water and cook until the peas are half cooked – they should be tender on the outside, but still firm in the middle. Allow the water to evaporate during cooking, until the pan is dry, but watch carefully and add a little extra water to prevent burning, if necessary.

4 Spread the peas out on to a tray, and when cool, grind to a paste and mix with the cumin and garlic.

5 Divide the dough into about 15 balls. Slightly flatten each ball of dough, put about 15ml/1 tbsp of mixture into the centre and fold over the edges to enclose the mixture.

6 Dust a rolling pin and a board with flour and roll out the dhal puri, taking care not to overstretch, until they are about 18cm/7in in diameter.

7 Heat a little oil on a tawa (roti pan) or in a heavy-based frying pan, swirling the oil to cover the base. Cook the dhal puris for about 3 minutes on each side until light brown. Fold them into a clean dish towel, to keep warm. Serve warm.

Fried Dumplins

Fried Dumplins are easy to make and the "sister" to Bakes, as they are also known in the Caribbean and Guyana. They are usually served with saltfish or fried fish, but they can be eaten quite simply with butter and jam or cheese. Children love them!

INGREDIENTS

Makes about 10
450g/1lb/4 cups self-raising flour
10ml/2 tsp sugar
2.5ml/½ tsp salt
300ml/½ pint/1¼ cups milk
oil, for frying

1 Sift the dry ingredients together into a large bowl, add the milk and mix and knead until smooth.

2 Divide the dough into ten balls, kneading each ball with floured hands. Press the balls gently to flatten into 7.5cm/3in rounds.

3 Heat a little oil in a non-stick frying pan until moderately hot. Place half the dumplins in the pan, reduce the heat to low and fry for about 15 minutes until they are golden brown, turning once.

4 Stand them on their sides for a few minutes to brown the edges, before removing them and draining on kitchen paper. Serve warm.

Pigeon Peas Cook-Up Rice

This Guyanese-style rice dish is made with the most commonly used peas.

INGREDIENTS

Serves 4–6

25g/1oz/2 tbsp butter or margarine
1 medium onion, chopped
1 garlic clove, crushed
25g/1oz/2 tbsp chopped spring onion
1 large carrot, diced
175g/6oz/about 1 cup pigeon peas
1 thyme sprig or 5ml/1 tsp dried thyme
1 cinnamon stick
600ml/1 pint/2½ cups vegetable stock
50g/2½oz/4 tbsp creamed coconut
1 hot chilli pepper, chopped
450g/1lb long grain rice
salt and freshly ground black pepper

1 Melt the butter or margarine in a large heavy saucepan, add the onion and garlic and sauté over a medium heat for 5 minutes, stirring occasionally.

2 Add the spring onion, carrot, pigeon peas, thyme, cinnamon, stock, creamed coconut, hot pepper and seasoning and bring to the boil.

3 Reduce the heat and then stir in the rice. Cover and simmer gently, over a low heat until all the liquid is absorbed and the rice is tender.

4 Stir with a fork to fluff up the rice before serving.

COOK'S TIP

Pigeon peas are also known as gunga peas. The fresh peas can be difficult to obtain, but you will find them in specialist shops. The frozen peas are green and the canned variety are brown. Drain the salted water from canned peas and rinse before using them in this recipe.

Green Bananas and Yam in Coconut Milk

INGREDIENTS

Serves 3–4

4 green bananas, peeled and halved
450g/1lb white yam, peeled and cut into pieces
1 thyme sprig
40g/1½oz creamed coconut
salt and freshly ground black pepper
chopped fresh thyme, and thyme sprigs, to garnish

1 Bring 900ml/1½ pints/3¾ cups water to the boil in a large saucepan, reduce the heat and add the green bananas and yam. Simmer gently for about 10 minutes.

2 Add the thyme, coconut and seasoning, bring back to the boil and cook over a moderate heat until the yam and banana are tender.

3 Transfer the yam and banana to a plate with a slotted spoon and continue cooking the coconut milk until thick and creamy.

4 When the sauce is ready, return vegetables to the pan and heat through. Spoon into a warmed serving dish, sprinkle with chopped thyme and garnish with thyme sprigs.

Cou-Cou

A Barbadian speciality that goes well with flying fish but can be served with any other fish, meat or vegetable stew.

INGREDIENTS

Serves 4

115g/4oz okra, topped, tailed and sliced
225g/8oz/1½ cups coarse cornmeal
600ml/1pint/2½ cups water or coconut milk
25g/1oz/2 tbsp butter
salt and freshly ground black pepper

1 Cook the okra in boiling water seasoned with a little salt and pepper for about 10 minutes. Drain and reserve the cooking liquid.

2 Bring half of the reserved liquid to the boil in a separate pan, add the okra and then beat in the cornmeal.

3 Cook on a very low heat, beating the mixture vigorously. Add the water or coconut milk, a little at a time, beating after each addition, to avoid it sticking to the bottom of the pan and burning.

4 Cover and cook for about 20 minutes, beating occasionally. When the cornmeal granules are soft the cou-cou is cooked, cover with foil and then a lid to keep moist and hot, until required. Spread the top with butter before serving.

Rice and Peas

This popular dish is also known as Peas and Rice on the islands in the Eastern Caribbean.

INGREDIENTS

Serves 6

175g/6oz/1 cup red kidney beans
2 fresh thyme sprigs
50g/2oz creamed coconut
2 bay leaves
1 onion, finely chopped
2 garlic cloves, crushed
2.5ml/½ tsp ground allspice
115g/4oz chopped red or green pepper
450g/1lb long grain rice
salt and freshly ground black pepper

1 Place the red kidney beans in a large bowl. Cover with water and leave to soak overnight.

2 Drain the beans, place in a large pan and add enough water to cover the beans by about 2.5cm/1in. Bring to the boil and boil over a high heat for 10 minutes, then reduce the heat and simmer for about 1½ hours or until the beans are tender.

3 Add the thyme, creamed coconut, bay leaves, onion, garlic, allspice, red or green pepper and seasoning and stir in 600ml/1 pint/2½ cups water.

4 Bring to the boil and add the rice. Stir well, reduce the heat and simmer, covered for 25–30 minutes, until all the liquid is absorbed. Serve as an accompaniment to fish, meat or vegetarian dishes.

Buttered Spinach and Rice

The layer of spinach was purely accidental – it was once missed from the dish and thus became a lovely topping for the rice!

INGREDIENTS

Serves 4
40g/1½oz/3 tbsp butter or margarine
1 onion, finely chopped
2 fresh tomatoes, chopped
450g/1lb basmati rice, washed
2 garlic cloves, crushed
600ml/1 pint/2½ cups stock or water
350g/12oz fresh spinach, shredded
salt and freshly ground black pepper
2 tomatoes, sliced, to garnish

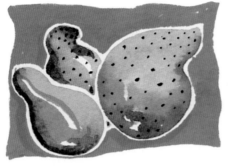

1 Melt 25g/1oz/2 tbsp of the butter or margarine in a large saucepan and fry the onion for a few minutes until soft. Add the chopped tomatoes and stir.

2 Add the rice and garlic, cook for 5 minutes, then gradually add the stock, stirring all the time. Season well.

3 Cover and simmer gently for 10–15 minutes until the rice is almost cooked, then reduce the heat to low.

4 Spread the spinach in a thick layer over the rice. Cover the pan and cook over a low heat for 5–8 minutes until the spinach has wilted. Dot the remaining butter over the top and then serve, garnished with sliced tomatoes.

--- COOK'S TIP ---

If fresh spinach is not available, you can use frozen leaf spinach instead. Thaw and drain 225g/8oz frozen spinach and cook as recipe for about 5 minutes. Finely shredded spring greens can also be used.

Creamed Sweet Potatoes

White sweet potatoes are best for this recipe, rather than orange sweet potatoes. White yams make a good substitute, especially poona (Ghanaian) yam.

INGREDIENTS

Serves 4
900g/2lb sweet potatoes
50g/2oz/4 tbsp butter
45ml/3 tbsp single cream
freshly grated nutmeg
15ml/1 tbsp snipped fresh chives
salt and freshly ground black pepper

1 Peel the sweet potatoes under cold running water and place in a bowl of salted water. Cut or slice them and place in a large saucepan and cover with cold water. Cook, covered for about 30 minutes.

2 When the potatoes are cooked, drain and add the butter, cream, nutmeg, chives and seasoning. Mash with a potato masher and then fluff up with a fork. Serve warm as an accompaniment to a curry or stew.

Corn Sticks

This recipe produces perfect corn bread in a loaf tin, or makes attractive corn sticks, if you can find the moulds.

INGREDIENTS

Makes 40 corn sticks
225g/8oz/2 cups plain flour
225g/8oz/1½ cups fine cornmeal
50ml/10 tsp baking powder
2.5ml/½ tsp salt
60ml/4 tbsp demerara sugar
450ml/¾ pint/1⅞ cups milk
2 eggs
50g/2oz/4 tbsp butter or margarine

1 Preheat the oven to 190°C/375°F/ Gas 5 and grease either corn bread moulds or a 900g/2lb loaf tin.

2 Sift together the flour, cornmeal, baking powder, salt and sugar into a large bowl. In a separate bowl, whisk the milk and eggs, then stir into the flour mixture.

3 Melt the butter or margarine in a small pan and stir into the mixture.

4 Spoon the mixture into the moulds or tin. Bake the corn sticks for 15 minutes. If using a loaf tin, bake for 30–35 minutes, until golden and hollow sounding when tapped.

COOK'S TIP

Because there is such a lot of baking powder, the cornmeal mixture begins to rise as soon as liquid is added, so bake straight away.

Fried Yellow Plantains

When plantains are yellow they are ripe and ready to enhance most meat, fish or vegetarian dishes. The riper the plantains the darker and sweeter they are.

INGREDIENTS

Serves 4
2 yellow plantains
oil, for shallow frying
finely snipped chives, to garnish

1 Using a small sharp knife, top and tail the plantains, and cut in half.

2 Slit the skin only, along the natural ridges of each piece of plantain.

3 Ease up the edge of the skin and run the tip of your thumb along the plantains, lifting the skin.

4 Peel away the skin and slice the plantains lengthways. Heat a little oil in a large frying pan and fry the plantain slices for 2–3 minutes each side until golden brown.

5 When the plantains are brown and crisp, drain on kitchen paper and serve hot or cold, sprinkled with finely snipped chives.

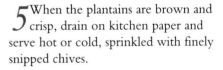

Okra Fried Rice

INGREDIENTS

Serves 3–4

30ml/2 tbsp vegetable oil
15ml/1 tbsp butter or margarine
1 garlic clove, crushed
½ red onion, finely chopped
115g/4oz okra, topped and tailed
30ml/2 tbsp diced green and red
  peppers
2.5ml/½ tsp dried thyme
2 green chillies, finely chopped
2.5ml/½ tsp five-spice powder
1 vegetable stock cube
30ml/2 tbsp soy sauce
15ml/1 tbsp chopped fresh
  coriander
225g/8oz/2½ cups cooked rice
salt and freshly ground black pepper
coriander sprigs, to garnish

1 Heat the oil and butter or margarine in a frying pan or wok, add the garlic and onion and cook over a moderate heat for 5 minutes until soft.

2 Thinly slice the okra, add to the pan or wok and sauté gently for 6–7 minutes.

3 Add the green and red peppers, thyme, chillies and five-spice powder and cook for 3 minutes, then crumble in the stock cube.

4 Add the soy sauce, coriander and rice and heat through, stirring well. Season with salt and pepper. Serve hot, garnished with coriander sprigs.

Aubergines with Garlic and Spring Onions

This is my favourite way of serving aubergines – you can make it even more delicious by adding little strips of smoked salmon at the last minute and letting them just warm through.

INGREDIENTS

Serves 4

45ml/3 tbsp vegetable oil
2 garlic cloves, crushed
3 tomatoes, peeled and chopped
900g/2lb aubergines, cut into
  chunks
150ml/¼ pint/⅔ cup vegetable stock
  or water
30ml/2 tbsp soy sauce
60ml/4 tbsp chopped spring onions
½ red pepper, chopped
1 hot chilli pepper, chopped
30ml/2 tbsp chopped fresh coriander
salt and freshly ground black pepper

1 Heat the oil in a wok or large frying pan and fry the garlic and tomatoes for a few minutes until slightly softened. Add the aubergines and toss together with the garlic and tomatoes.

2 Add the stock or water and cover the pan. Simmer gently until the aubergines are very soft. Stir in the soy sauce and half of the spring onions.

3 Add the red pepper, hot chilli pepper and seasoning to the pan and stir well.

4 Stir in the coriander and sprinkle with the rest of the spring onion.

CAKES, DESSERTS AND DRINKS

Tropical fruits and nuts flavored with spices are the basis of many of the recipes in this section. In the Caribbean, people eat fresh fruits and nuts "au naturel" at any time of day. However, both fresh and dried fruits are also used widely in desserts, cakes, and homemade breads as well as in a variety of superb fruit drinks, alcoholic cocktails and punches. Nowadays, almost all popular Caribbean fruits can be found throughout the year in most large supermarkets and West Indian delicatessens. If fresh fruit is not available, then use canned fruit instead.

Caribbean Fruit and Rum Cake

My mother's recipe for a cake that is eaten at Christmas, weddings and other special occasions. It is known as Black Cake, because, traditionally, the recipe usually uses burnt sugar.

INGREDIENTS

Makes 1 cake

450g/1lb/2 cups currants
450g/1lb/3 cups raisins
225g/8oz/1 cup prunes, stoned
115g/4oz/⅔ cup mixed peel
400g/14oz/2¼ cups dark soft brown
   sugar
5ml/1 tsp mixed spice
90ml/6 tbsp rum, plus more if needed
300ml/½ pint/1¼ cups sherry, plus
   more if needed
450g/1lb/2 cups softened butter
10 eggs, beaten
450g/1lb/4 cups self-raising flour
5ml/1 tsp vanilla essence

1 Wash the currants, raisins, prunes and mixed peel, then pat dry. Place in a food processor and process until finely chopped. Transfer to a large, clean jar or bowl, add 115g/4oz of the sugar, the mixed spice, rum and sherry. Mix very well and then cover with a lid and set aside for anything from 2 weeks to 3 months – the longer it is left, the better the flavour will be.

2 Stir the fruit mixture occasionally and keep covered, adding more alcohol, if you like.

3 Preheat the oven to 160°C/325°F/ Gas 3. Grease and line a 25cm/10in round cake tin with a double layer of greaseproof paper.

4 Sift the flour, and set aside. Cream together the butter and remaining sugar and beat in the eggs until the mixture is smooth and creamy.

5 Add the fruit mixture, then gradually stir in the flour and vanilla essence. Mix well, adding 15–30ml/1–2 tbsp sherry if the mixture is too stiff; it should just fall off the back of the spoon, but should not be too runny.

6 Spoon the mixture into the prepared tin, cover loosely with foil and bake for about 2½ hours until the cake is firm and springy. Leave to cool in the tin overnight, then sprinkle with more rum if the cake is not to be used immediately. Wrap the cake in foil to keep it moist.

COOK'S TIP

Although the dried fruits are chopped in a food processor, they can be marinated whole, if preferred. If you don't have enough time to marinate the fruit, simmer the fruit in the alcohol mixture for about 30 minutes, and leave overnight.

Barbadian Coconut Sweet Bread

Often made at Christmas time, this delicious coconut bread is most enjoyable with a cup of hot chocolate or a glass of fruit punch.

INGREDIENTS

Makes 1 large or two small loaves
175g/6oz/³⁄₄ cup butter or margarine
115g/4oz/²⁄₃ cup demerara sugar
225g/8oz/2 cups self-raising flour
200g/7oz/scant 2 cups plain flour
115g/4oz desiccated coconut
5ml/1 tsp mixed spice
10ml/2 tsp vanilla essence
15ml/1 tbsp rum (optional)
2 eggs
about 150ml/¹⁄₄ pint/²⁄₃ cup milk
15ml/1 tbsp caster sugar, blended with
   30ml/2 tbsp water, to glaze

1 Preheat the oven to 180°C/350°F/ Gas 4. Grease two 450g/1lb loaf tins or one 900g/2lb tin.

2 Place the butter or margarine and sugar in a large bowl and sift in the flour. Rub the ingredients together with your fingertips until the mixture resembles fine breadcrumbs.

3 Add the coconut, mixed spice, vanilla essence, rum if using, eggs and milk and mix together well with your hands. If the mixture is too dry, moisten with milk. Knead on a floured board until firm and pliable.

4 Halve the mixture and place in the prepared loaf tins. Glaze with sugared water and bake for 1 hour until the loaves are cooked. The loaves are ready when a skewer comes out clean.

Duckanoo

This tasty pudding originated in west Africa.

INGREDIENTS

Serves 4–6

450g/1lb/3 cups fine cornmeal
350g/12oz fresh coconut, chopped
600ml/1 pint/2½ cups fresh milk
115g/4oz currants or raisins
50g/2oz/4 tbsp butter or margarine, melted
115g/4oz/½ cup demerara sugar
60ml/4 tbsp water
1.5ml/¼ tsp freshly grated nutmeg
2.5ml/½ tsp ground cinnamon
5ml/1 tsp vanilla essence

1 Place the cornmeal in a large bowl. Blend the coconut and the milk in a blender or food processor until smooth. Stir the coconut mixture into the cornmeal, then add all the remaining ingredients and stir well.

2 Take 6 pieces of foil and fold into 13 x 15cm/5 x 6in pockets leaving an opening on one short side. Fold the edges of the remaining sides tightly to ensure that they are well sealed.

3 Put one or two spoonfuls of the mixture into each pocket and fold over the edge of the foil to seal.

4 Place the foil pockets in a large saucepan of boiling water. Cover and simmer for about 45–60 minutes. Lift out the pockets from the water and remove the foil. Serve the duckanoo by themselves or with fresh cream.

Apple and Cinnamon Crumble Cake

This scrumptious cake has layers of spicy fruit and crumble and is quite delicious served warm with fresh cream.

INGREDIENTS

Makes 1 cake
3 large cooking apples
2.5ml/½ tsp ground cinnamon
250g/9oz/1 cup butter
250g/9oz/1¼ cups caster sugar
4 eggs
450g/1lb/4 cups self-raising flour

For the crumble topping
175g/6oz/¾ cup demerara sugar
125g/4¼oz/1¼ cups plain flour
5ml/1 tsp ground cinnamon
65g/2½oz/about 4½ tbsp desiccated
   coconut
115g/4oz/½ cup butter

1 Preheat the oven to 180°C/350°F/ Gas 4. Grease a 25cm/10in round cake tin and line the base with greaseproof paper. To make the crumble topping, mix together the sugar, flour, cinnamon and coconut in a bowl, then rub in the butter with your fingertips and set aside.

2 Peel and core the apples, then grate them coarsely. Place them in a bowl, sprinkle with the cinnamon and set aside.

3 Cream the butter and sugar in a bowl with an electric mixer, until light and fluffy. Beat in the eggs, one at a time, beating well after each addition.

4 Sift in half the flour, mix well, then add the remaining flour and stir until smooth.

5 Spread half the cake mixture evenly over the base of the prepared tin. Spoon the apples on top and scatter over half the crumble topping.

6 Spread the remaining cake mixture over the crumble and finally top with the remaining crumble topping.

7 Bake for 1 hour 10 minutes – 1 hour 20 minutes, covering the cake with foil if it browns too quickly. Leave in the tin for about 5 minutes, before turning out on to a wire rack. Once cool, cut into slices to serve.

COOK'S TIP

To make the topping in a food processor, add all the ingredients and process for a few seconds until the mixture resembles bread-crumbs. You can also grate the apples using the grating disc. If you don't have a 25cm/10in round tin you can use a 20cm/8in square cake tin.

Bread and Butter Custard

This dessert is a delicious family favourite. A richer version can be made with fresh cream, instead of evaporated milk. It can also be made using other dried fruit – mango is particularly good.

INGREDIENTS

Serves 4
15ml/1 tbsp softened butter
3 thin slices of bread, crusts removed
400g/14oz can evaporated milk
150ml/¼ pint/⅔ cup fresh milk
2.5ml/½ tsp mixed spice
40g/1½oz/3 tbsp demerara sugar
2 eggs, whisked
75g/3oz/½ cup sultanas
freshly grated nutmeg
a little icing sugar, for dusting

1 Preheat the oven to 180°C/350°F/ Gas 4 and lightly butter an ovenproof dish. Butter the bread and cut into small pieces.

2 Lay the buttered bread in several layers in the prepared dish.

3 Whisk together the evaporated milk and the fresh milk, mixed spice, sugar and eggs in a large bowl. Pour the mixture over the bread and butter. Sprinkle over the sultanas and leave to stand for 30 minutes.

4 Grate a little nutmeg over the top and bake for 30–40 minutes until the custard is just set and golden. Serve sprinkled with icing sugar.

Avocado Salad in Ginger and Orange Sauce

This is an unusual fruit salad since avocado is more often treated as a vegetable. However, in the Caribbean it is used as a fruit, which of course it is!

INGREDIENTS

Serves 4
2 firm ripe avocados
3 firm ripe bananas, chopped
12 fresh cherries or strawberries
juice of 1 large orange
shredded fresh root ginger (optional)

For the ginger syrup
50g/2oz fresh root ginger, chopped
900ml/1½ pints/3¾ cups water
225g/8oz/1 cup demerara sugar
2 cloves

1 First make the ginger syrup; place the ginger, water, sugar and cloves in a saucepan and bring to the boil. Reduce the heat and simmer for about 1 hour, until well reduced and syrupy.

2 Remove the ginger and discard. Leave to cool. Store in a covered, clean container in the fridge.

3 Peel the avocados, cut into cubes and place in a bowl with the bananas and cherries or strawberries.

4 Pour the orange juice over the fruits. Add 60ml/4 tbsp of the ginger syrup and mix gently, using a metal spoon. Chill for 30 minutes and add a little shredded ginger, if using.

Fruits of the Tropics Salad

INGREDIENTS

Serves 4–6

1 medium pineapple

400g/14oz can guava halves in syrup

2 medium bananas, sliced

1 large mango, peeled, stoned and
    diced

115g/4oz stem ginger and 30ml/2 tbsp
    of the syrup

60ml/4 tbsp thick coconut milk

10ml/2 tsp sugar

2.5ml/½ tsp freshly grated nutmeg

2.5ml/½ tsp ground cinnamon

strips of coconut, to decorate

1 Peel, core and cube the pineapple, and place in a serving bowl. Drain the guavas, reserve the syrup and chop. Add the guavas to the bowl with one of the bananas and the mango.

2 Chop the stem ginger and add to the pineapple mixture.

3 Pour 30ml/2 tbsp of the ginger syrup, and the reserved guava syrup into a blender or food processor and add the other banana, the coconut milk and the sugar. Blend to make a smooth creamy purée.

4 Pour the banana and coconut mixture over the fruit, add a little grated nutmeg and a sprinkling of cinnamon. Serve chilled, decorated with strips of coconut.

Coconut Ice Cream

An easy-to-make, quite heavenly, ice cream that will be loved by all for its tropical taste.

INGREDIENTS

Serves 8

400g/14oz can evaporated milk
400g/14oz can condensed milk
400g/14oz can coconut milk
freshly grated nutmeg
5ml/1 tsp almond essence
lemon balm sprigs, lime slices and
   shredded coconut, to decorate

1 Mix together the evaporated, condensed and coconut milks in a large freezerproof bowl and stir in the nutmeg and almond essence.

2 Chill in a freezer for an hour or two until the mixture is semi-frozen.

3 Remove from the freezer and whisk the mixture with a hand or electric whisk until it is fluffy and almost doubled in volume.

4 Pour into a freezer container, then cover and freeze. Soften slightly before serving, decorated with lemon balm, lime slices and shredded coconut.

Spiced Pineapple Punch

INGREDIENTS

Serves 3–4

1.5 litres/2½ pints/6¼ cups pineapple
   juice
400g/14oz can condensed milk
5ml/1 tsp vanilla essence
freshly grated nutmeg
pinch of ground cinnamon
lime juice, to serve

—— COOK'S TIP ——

If you don't have a blender or food processor,
just pour the pineapple juice and milk into a
large bowl and whisk vigorously to mix.

1 Pour the pineapple juice into a blender or food processor. Add all of the condensed milk and the vanilla essence and process for a few seconds, until the juice and milk are well blended.

2 Add the grated nutmeg and cinnamon and blend for a few more seconds. Chill the punch until very cold and serve with ice and a squeeze of lime.

Sarah's Island Mist Fruit Punch

Memories of sipping refreshing
fruity punch and feasting on
mangoes in the St Lucian hills on
beautiful misty mornings
provided the inspiration for this
delicious drink.

INGREDIENTS

Serves 3–4

2 bananas
60ml/4 tbsp ginger syrup
2.5ml/½ tsp almond essence
2.5ml/½ tsp vanilla essence
1 litre/1¾ pints/4 cups mango juice
750ml/1¼ pints/3⅔ cups pineapple
   juice
250ml/8fl oz/1 cup lemonade
freshly grated nutmeg
lemon balm and orange slices,
   to decorate

—— COOK'S TIP ——

Prepare this punch up to 2 hours in
advance and chill until ready to serve.

1 Peel the bananas and chop them into 1cm/½in pieces.

2 Blend the bananas, ginger syrup and essences in a blender or food processor until smooth.

3 Transfer the mixture to a large punch bowl. Stir in the mango and pineapple juices, then pour in the lemonade. Finish by sprinkling in some grated nutmeg. Serve chilled, decorated with lemon balm and orange slices.

Demerara Rum Punch

The inspiration for this punch came from the rum distillery at Plantation Diamond Estate in Guyana where some of the finest rum in the world is made, and the tantalizing aromas of sugar cane and rum pervade the air.

INGREDIENTS

Serves 4

150ml/¼ pint/⅔ cup orange juice
150ml/¼ pint/⅔ cup pineapple juice
150ml/¼ pint/⅔ cup mango juice
120ml/4fl oz/½ cup water
250ml/8fl oz/1 cup dark rum
a shake of angostura bitters
freshly grated nutmeg
25g/1oz/2 tbsp demerara sugar
1 small banana
1 large orange

1 Pour the orange, pineapple and mango juices into a large punch bowl. Stir in the water.

2 Add the rum, angostura bitters, nutmeg and sugar. Stir gently for a few minutes until the sugar has dissolved.

3 Slice the banana and stir gently into the punch.

4 Slice the orange and add to the punch. Chill and serve with ice.

COOK'S TIP

You can use white rum instead of dark, if you prefer. To make a stronger punch, add more rum.

Caribbean Cream Stout Punch

A well-known "pick-me-up" that is popular all over the Caribbean.

INGREDIENTS

Serves 2

475ml/16fl oz/2 cups stout
300ml/½ pint/1¼ cups evaporated milk
75ml/5 tbsp condensed milk
75ml/5 tbsp sherry
2 or 3 drops vanilla essence
freshly grated nutmeg

1 Mix together the stout, evaporated and condensed milks, sherry and vanilla essence in a blender or food processor, or whisk together in a large mixing bowl, until creamy.

2 Add a little grated nutmeg to the stout mixture and blend or whisk again for a few minutes.

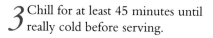

3 Chill for at least 45 minutes until really cold before serving.

Index